Bravo!

Other books by Alan Goldhamer, DC
The Health Promoting Cookbook

with Douglas J. Lisle, PhD
The Pleasure Trap

HEALTH-PROMOTING MEALS FROM THE TRUENORTH KITCHEN

Bravo!

RAMSES BRAVO

INTRODUCTION BY
ALAN GOLDHAMER, DC
DIRECTOR, TRUENORTH HEALTH CENTER

BOOK PUBLISHING COMPANY
SUMMERTOWN, TENNESSEE

Cover and interior design: Scattaregia Design
Cover and interior photos: Warren Jefferson
Food styling: Barbara Jefferson

ISBN 13: 978-1-57067-269-9

18 17 16 15 14 13 12   1 2 3 4 5 6 7 8 9

Book Publishing Company
PO Box 99
Summertown, TN 38483
888-260-8458
bookpubco.com

Library of Congress Cataloging-in-Publication Data

Bravo, Ramses.
  Bravo! : vegan recipes from the Truenorth Health Center / Ramses Bravo ; foreword by T. Colin Campbell.
     p. cm.
  Includes index.
  ISBN 978-1-57067-269-9 (pbk.) -- ISBN 978-1-57067-941-4 (e-book)
  1. Vegan cooking. 2. Vegans. I. Title.
  TX837.B756 2012
  641.5'636--dc23
                          2011051704

Printed on recycled paper

Book Publishing Company is a member of Green Press Initiative. We chose to print this title on paper with 100% postconsumer recycled content, processed without chlorine, which saved the following natural resources:

• 34 trees
• 976 pounds of solid waste
• 15,402 gallons of water
• 3,416 pounds of greenhouse gases
• 14 million BTU of energy

For more information on Green Press Initiative, visit www.greenpressinitiative.org.
Environmental impact estimates were made using the Environmental Defense Fund Paper Calculator edf.org/papercalculator.

On the front cover: **Hawaiian Salad**, p. 64, with **Mango–Ginger Dressing**, p. 68
On the back cover: **Breakfast Potatoes**, p. 44; **Red Lentil Loaf**, p. 96, with **Bell Pepper Coulis**, p. 113, and **Oven-Roasted Tomatoes with Arugula**, p. 79; and **Peach-Blueberry Crisp**, p. 127

Contents

Lulu, I love you . . . never too much.

Logan, I hope to meet and play with you in heaven some day.

April, thank you for all the great memories.

Mom and Dad, thank you for all your support and encouragement.

Mama Rosita, you are the reason I have a passion for cooking.

Foreword

I SPEAK BOTH FROM A PERSONAL AND A PROFESSIONAL PERSPECTIVE regarding this book, *Bravo!*, and TrueNorth Health Center. I have spent time at the center on three separate occasions, and several of my family members, friends, and acquaintances have also visited. In addition, my colleagues and I have analyzed the center's data on hypertension that led to two coauthored, peer-reviewed publications.

The food and health information offered at the center is as good as it gets. I have eaten the food, attended many of the lectures, read their material, and now feel confident that I know quite well the basis of their information. There is none better. The center is a very professional institution founded on very sound science, and it shows at every level.

I also have learned much from the TrueNorth staff professionals, especially in their understanding of the body's ability to heal itself, if the right nutrition, resources, and experiences are provided. Conventional allopathic medicine fails to acknowledge this exceptional activity, both in the medical research laboratory and in the practicing clinic. The medical staff at True-North, under the leadership of director Alan Goldhamer, has developed a fairly unique food-based treatment strategy for their patients and has demonstrated exceptional health restorative benefits. This strategy, which begins with a variable period of medically supervised water-only fasting for many patients, culminates with the consumption of food that restores and maintains health.

Although this is a provocative approach for many professionals trained in conventional medicine, it is time that it be aired. Providing people with the kinds of recipes that achieve the amazing benefits that are routinely produced at TrueNorth is a great way to get this information in the hands of the public.

I highly recommend this book and its recipes—they can save your life.

—T. Colin Campbell, PhD
    professor emeritus of nutritional biochemistry,
    Cornell University

Preface

PREPARING AND SERVING FOOD ARE HALLOWED TRADITIONS ALL AROUND THE WORLD. Every nationality has its own recognizable cuisine, made up of unique foods and recipes. Sometimes these recipes are more of a tribute to human ingenuity than optimal nutrition. Traditionally, people simply made the best meals they could with whatever was available in their climate and region. And, considering these limitations and the limited capacity for storage and importation, they did a pretty tasty job of it.

Today, people are beginning to realize that there is more to a good diet than mere tastiness. We want our meals to be healthful too, but that can be a challenge. How do you make foods that look and taste good without adding unhealthful oil, salt, and sugar? That important question is what inspired me to write this book. I decided to create delicious, easy-to-make, wholesome recipes so people wouldn't have to choose between tasty foods and healthful foods, meal after meal.

I created almost one hundred vegan recipes for this book to help you prepare and enjoy delicious meals and get (and stay) healthy. I wrote this book with the goal of providing the very best, most healthful recipes for people who want to transform their lives, so all my recipes are vegan.

Changing Your Diet

If you are not healthy, if you lack vigor, if you are overweight, or if you just need a positive change in your life, this book is for you. The recipes and food tips will make your dietary transition as easy as possible. I planned it that way. Why? Because not too long ago, like many hardworking chefs, I was run-down, overweight, and out of sorts myself. Let me explain what happened.

I always loved to eat, and as a young boy I spent endless hours in my grandmother's kitchen. I relished the chance to help her prepare meals, especially chiles rellenos, my favorite. When she made chicken soup, I gobbled up the boiled chicken skin—and not only the skin from my bowl but also the skin from everyone else's bowls. Does it surprise you to learn that I was a chubby kid?

While still in high school, I decided to turn my passion for food into a profession. After graduation, I enrolled at City College in San Francisco and received my degree in hotel and restaurant management in 1998. Afterward, I worked at a number of exclusive resorts, including four years as executive chef at the Kenwood Inn and Spa in Kenwood, California. I was steadily achieving professional success. Unfortunately, my waistline was growing steadily too. Like most chefs, I worked in restaurants and hotels where healthful meals were not a priority. I ate anything and everything. When I left my last hotel job, I was out of shape, overweight, and exhausted from the long work hours. On my days off, instead of enjoying time with my family, all I wanted to do was rest.

Fortunately, I learned about a remarkable place, TrueNorth Health Center in Santa Rosa, California, where only the finest and most healthful food is served. They were looking for an executive chef, and I was looking for a new challenge. And I knew that this would be a challenge. In fact, I came very close to not taking the job. I thought I would be signing up for an impossible task. How could I prepare meals all day long without all the ingredients I was used to? Wouldn't the food be too bland? In the end, I decided to take the job, but I wasn't entirely optimistic. I thought maybe I'd learn something, and if it didn't work out, I could always find another job. I'm happy to say it has more than worked out: it has changed my life.

I've been at TrueNorth for four years now, creating and developing exquisite vegan cuisine using the same approach I used so successfully at my previous jobs—combining simple flavors and textures that complement each other. My love for eating and cooking is as strong as ever. It's simply being directed in a much more healthful direction. The response from the guests has been most gratifying. Eating this way does wonders. I've seen thousands of people restore their health. On average, TrueNorth guests lose two pounds each week while eating the types of meals described in this book.

If you need to transform your diet or health right away, consider a stay at TrueNorth Health Center today. Call 707-586-5555 or visit HealthPromoting.com. That way, you can make immediate changes, and you won't have to worry about making meals. I'll make them for you.

As for me, I'm a new man. I've lost weight, and my energy level is higher than ever. I work out or go running during my lunch break, and my daughter and I often go on bike rides together. This new quality of life is priceless, and I am deeply appreciative. One way of showing that appreciation is offering this book to you along with my promise: as you transform your diet and health, you will experience more joy and happiness than you ever thought possible.

Acknowledgments

I WANT TO THANK MY FAMILY FOR ALWAYS NURTURING AND SUPPORTING ME in my endeavors, the teachers and fellow chefs who gave me the opportunities to learn and grow in my profession, and doctors Alan Goldhamer and Jennifer Marano and the staff and guests of TrueNorth Health Center, who have served as food critics and taste testers as I mastered the art and science of healthful cuisine.

I also would like to thank Laurie Masters for her nutritional analyses of the recipes, Carissa and Bradley for helping give shape to this book, Jim Lennon and Susan Taylor Lennon for their thoughtful editing, and Cynthia Holzapfel and Jo Stepaniak at Book Publishing Company for guiding this project through completion. Without all of your help, this book would not have been possible.

Bravo!

Introduction

HERE'S A JOKE THAT'S BEEN MAKING THE ROUNDS SINCE VAUDEVILLE DAYS. A man goes to his doctor and says: "It hurts when I do this." The doctor replies: "Then don't do that." You've probably heard this one, and it may have made you chuckle. But have you ever stopped to think that we laugh at jokes when we recognize their kernel of truth? Perhaps on some level we know that avoiding pain and illness may be exquisitely simple. What if, to stop hurting, we just need to stop what we're doing?

Surprisingly, many of us don't know what we need to stop doing to feel better. Furthermore, neither do our doctors. Like the patient in this joke, we're unlikely to get the thoughtful attention that we deserve, and we're likely to get insufficient answers. Naturally, our frustration grows when we don't know how to get better, let alone how to avoid disease before it even starts. What we and our doctors need to understand is that health is the natural, spontaneous consequence of healthful living. It is rarely the result of pharmaceuticals or expensive or complicated medical care.

In the United States and other developed countries, most people eat extraordinarily unhealthful diets. Witness the national epidemics of cancer, diabetes, heart disease, and obesity. Unknowingly, we are hooked on foods that cause these conditions, which are sometimes referred to as the "diseases of excess." Yet we fail to recognize food as a major cause of these illnesses. For far too many people, the singular act of eating the standard American diet leads to devastating results.

T. Colin Campbell, PhD, coauthor of *The China Study* and author of the foreword to this book, has revealed just how damaging certain foods can be, despite our society's enthusiasm for them. Campbell grew up on a dairy farm, and he and his family ate typical American fare, including meat and a lot of dairy products. He began his career looking for more efficient ways to develop animal protein. Over time, however, his research unexpectedly took him in the opposite direction. Now he warns people against consuming animal-based foods. Through their research, Campbell and his colleagues came to believe that animal protein is a major culprit in cancer development. They also discovered that the primary protein in dairy products—casein—appears to be an aggressive cancer promoter.

Eliminating animal-based foods does more than help us avoid cancer. This choice also helps us steer clear of heart and atherosclerotic disease. For example, people who abstain from eating animal-based foods have cholesterol levels that are 35 percent lower than those who don't. Extensive research has also shown that people with a cholesterol level under 150 rarely suffer a heart attack. In addition, a plant-based, whole-foods diet can reverse a host of chronic health problems, including diabetes and obesity.

Subtract Your Way to Health

The recipes in this book, and the delicious meals that we serve at TrueNorth Health Center, are designed with your optimum health in mind. They contain no meat, fish, fowl, eggs, or dairy products. In addition, they contain no processed oils, refined carbohydrates, salt, or sugar. What's left, you might wonder. Instead of animal-based foods, processed products, and refined ingredients, we offer real foods packed with flavor and nutrition that promote health: fresh fruits and vegetables, whole grains, legumes, nuts, and seeds. Without harmful products tearing down our health, and with whole, nutritious foods building us back up, the body naturally regains its health.

The notion of removing foods from our diets to improve health may seem surprising, because it contradicts the Western view that we should "take something" to feel better. Modern medicine often leads both the physician and the patient to look for health solutions in all the wrong places. In the vast majority of cases, the conclusion reached is that something is "missing" and needs to be "added," typically in the form of a prescription drug. The fact is, most modern-day health problems are the result of dietary excesses. Adding more pills to our health-care regimen is not our only or even our best option. What we need to do is stop eating the foods that are making us sick.

End Your Addiction to Harmful Foods

Blame our ancestors for our built-in dietary preferences. Over millennia, they faced a problem that is unfamiliar to most of us today. Whereas we live in an environment of excess, where groceries virtually spill out of the stores and into the streets, they experienced scarcity on a regular basis. Even now, there are hunter-gatherer societies for whom a slight change in food availability could bring demise.

Miraculously, each of us is the result of countless generations of people who managed to get enough to eat and survived under some very harsh conditions. To persevere in an environment of scarcity, our ancestors depended on higher-calorie foods—ones that are naturally high in fats and sugars. Early humans did not live on roots and shoots alone; they ate fruits, nuts, seeds, and small game, if they could get their hands on it. Complex mechanisms of brain chemistry attracted them to these calorie-rich and pleasurable foods, which would help to ensure their survival in times of scarcity.

Because this collective memory and survival instinct was passed from generation to generation, our innate preference even now is to fill up on high-calorie foods, although we no longer live in "survival mode." Understandably, today's diet—artificially concentrated with animal-based proteins, oils, and sugar and other refined carbohydrates—appeals to us deeply. It seems to be the answer to our primordial prayer. But our ancient programming has become obsolete. In an environment of abundance, our instinctive preference for and overconsumption of high-calorie foods has come to do us more harm than good, leading many of us to suffer unnecessarily, and gravely, as a consequence.

We also are programmed to be more concerned about deficiencies than we are about excesses. After all, throughout human history, dietary deficiencies were common, while dietary excesses were rare. Psychologically, we find it difficult to accept that our bounty is killing us.

In addition, we fail to appreciate just how drastically our diets and tastes differ from those of even our recent ancestors. The modern American diet is largely built around processed foods. They have taste-stimulating capacities that far exceed those of the whole, natural foods that people used to eat, and our preferences have adapted to this unnatural stimulation. To us, this food tastes "normal," because we have forgotten what real food tastes like.

Beyond being accustomed to highly artificial flavors, we are inherently attracted to certain types of foods, and their ready availability and easy accessibility have caused us to become addicted to them. Some of the most unhealthful selections—including cheese and other dairy products, meat, and sugar—produce the same biochemical response as a class of drugs called opiates, which includes morphine and heroin. Food, like drugs, can stimulate the pleasure center of the brain. Anybody who has ever needed a chocolate fix can attest to that.

While we crave the pleasure that food can give us, we simultaneously follow our instincts to conserve energy. Like other animals, we are designed by nature to seek the greatest rewards with the least amount of effort. In essence, we are programmed to make the most efficient use of the food and fuel that was so scarce for our ancestors. As a result, we now find ourselves in an environment in which it is exceptionally easy to make not only unhealthful but also harmful choices. For example, fast food is a convenient and seductive option. Taking a detour to the drive-through means that getting dinner on the table can require little thought, modest expense, and almost no effort. This scenario is significantly more appealing to our energy-conservation programming than the prospect of preparing a health-promoting meal.

Clearly, our ancestors passed along internal messages that ensured their survival but work against us in modern times, making us less likely to choose the most beneficial foods. This disadvantage is compounded by the powerful external messages we receive from advertisements, product placement, and other marketing techniques that take advantage of our instinctive urges and drive our behavior in the wrong direction. The greatest reason that we don't eat right may be this: Food is big business. The more we eat and the less the food costs to produce, the more profits there are to be made by manufacturers, investors, and, yes, even the medical profession. Consequently, we are constantly bombarded with misleading information about food and health.

Defy Common Food Myths

A significant portion of the food industry's advertising budget is devoted to dubious claims about our "need" to eat various unhealthful products, especially animal-based foods. We are told that unless we regularly consume ample amounts of dairy products, eggs, fish and fish oil, and meat, we won't get the vitamins, minerals, proteins, or fats we need. Why does the food industry push these messages? Because compared to vegetables and other plant-based foods, these animal-based foods are highly profitable. When companies churn out artificially flavored convenience foods with these ingredients, we readily fall into their trap and boost their profits even more. Let's set the record straight: plant-based foods, eaten in sufficient quantities, provide everything we need with the exception of vitamin B_{12}, which can easily be obtained from a supplement.

As long as we get enough calories from a wide variety of whole, natural foods to meet our weight and energy requirements, we will not only meet our nutrient needs, but we will also be dramatically better nourished than if we were eating only the "best" of the typical American diet. Contrary to popular food mythology, the issue is not whether it is possible to maintain health without eating animal protein, fat, oil, salt, and sugar, but rather, whether it is possible to maintain health while eating them.

Animal Protein

The most pervasive food myth is that eating animal protein is necessary for our health. When you switch to a plant-based diet, you will invariably be asked this question repeatedly: "Where do you get your protein?" Our culture has been inculcated with the notion that animal protein is the ultimate nutrient. The idea is so prevalent, most people don't even realize that plant-based foods are also rich in protein or that animal-based foods aren't particularly high in protein per calorie: dark leafy greens, such as chard, collard greens, kale, and spinach, win that prize. Because leafy greens are low in calories, other protein-rich plant foods—legumes, such as beans and lentils; whole grains, such as brown rice and quinoa; and nuts and seeds—can help round out all our needs.

The bottom line is that animal-based foods have an undeserved reputation as being a superior source of protein. However, as a source of saturated fat and cholesterol, they have earned their place as well-recognized health threats, contributing to heart disease and other problems.

Calcium and Dairy Products

It's true that our bodies need a certain amount of calcium for bone health, as extensive advertising by the dairy industry has alerted us for decades. However, we don't need to rely on dairy products as a source of calcium. Green vegetables, beans, and other plant-based foods provide plenty. Vegetables such as broccoli and kale contain calcium that is more absorbable than the calcium from animal-based foods. In addition, plant-based foods provide potassium and numerous other bone-building nutrients.

In Japan, China, and some parts of Africa, people don't traditionally consume dairy products, and they have healthy bones. Moreover, in those countries fractures due to thinning bones or osteoporosis are much rarer than in the United States.

If you are worried about osteoporosis, let me remind you that subtracting harmful foods is the key to health. Calcium loss, and ultimately thinning bones, stems from eating diets high in salt and animal-based foods. Avoiding these will help you retain calcium in your bones; adding calcium supplements or dairy products is not the answer.

Fats and Oils

The harmfulness of certain fats, especially trans fats and saturated fats, is so great that almost everyone knows they should be avoided. But consuming even small amounts of refined oils—including olive oil and other fats that are touted as healthful—can contribute to obesity and clogged arteries. Food industry myths about fats abound. The manufacturers of fish oil supplements promote their products as the answer to meeting our omega-3 and omega-6 fatty acid needs. Thankfully for our health (and breath), we can meet our essential fatty acid needs simply by eating plant-based foods. Dark leafy greens and avocados, plus small amounts of nuts (especially walnuts) and seeds (especially ground flaxseeds), can provide all the healthful fats we need.

Salt and Sugar

Salt and sugar are two substances that send our taste buds into a frenzy. Have a little, and we'll want a lot. However, adding salt to food can lead to major health risks. Excess sodium is associated with serious conditions, including high blood pressure, heart attack, osteoporosis, stomach cancer, and stroke. All the sodium and other important minerals we need are contained in whole, natural foods. Don't be deceived by "health food" industry advertising. Salt is salt. It doesn't matter if it comes from the mine or the sea, or if it is blessed by your guru's guru. Adding salt to your food is almost always a harmful practice.

Most added sugars are empty calories (calories without appreciable nutrients). Sugars are dangerous because they lack the nutrients we need to build health, and because they are easy to overeat. If you are eating too many calories (whether from added sugars or from any other source), you will become overweight, and we know that being overweight is a risk factor for many diseases. All the healthful sugars we need are contained in appropriate amounts in whole, natural foods.

Refined Carbohydrates

Many so-called diet books have irresponsibly warned us to beware the dreaded carbohydrate. The fact is, carbohydrates are necessary. Beans, fruits, vegetables, and whole grains are carbohydrates, and they are the foundation of a healthful diet. However, *refined* carbohydrates, which are abundant in the processed foods that are churned out by the food industry today, are what we should fear.

There are three main drawbacks to eating refined carbohydrates or starches such as wheat flour and other flours. First, wheat flour contains gluten, the protein that gives bread dough its body. Many people are allergic to gluten to some degree, often without knowing it. Second, the outer coat of a whole grain is stripped when it is made into refined flour, and fiber is lost. Fiber is essential for normal bowel function and maintaining the "friendly" bacteria in our intestines. Third, even when whole grains are ground into whole-grain flour, their calorie density per mouthful is increased. The milled grain, because it is more condensed, actually has more calories per measure than the whole grain! This makes it hard for our brains to calculate how many calories the body is taking in, which can lead to overeating. In part, the body determines satiety by the volume of food in the stomach. However, foods can be similar in volume but not in calories. When we eat a large volume of high-calorie foods, we are not likely to notice that we're getting more calories than we need. Refined foods, and wheat flour in particular, can deceive the body in this regard. So while a few recipes in this book call for rice flour or oat flour, no recipes call for wheat flour.

A final word about wheat flour: The term "whole wheat" is mistakenly thought to be synonymous with "wholesome." For example, the average consumer typically thinks that breads and pastries that include *some* whole wheat flour (regardless of the other ingredients) are more healthful than virtually identical products that don't. Add the word "organic" to the mix and even more confusion abounds. Regardless of whether refined products contain a small amount of a whole food or were organically grown, they are still health-harming and have little nutritional value.

Moderation

When it comes to making healthful changes, one of the most dangerous beliefs is that any food is acceptable provided it is eaten in moderation. Another common but equally dangerous belief is that we should begin with modest changes and slowly build toward success. The truth is that, to break free of the insidious hold that unhealthful foods have on us, we need to make revolutionary changes if we want revolutionary results. If we hold on to the idea that it's okay to sneak a few French fries or sip the occasional milkshake, we will retain our tastes for these foods, and they will retain their power over us. My advice is to make a clean break from unhealthful foods and commit to sweeping, simultaneous changes to achieve optimum health.

Find True North

"Finding true north" means finding your way. For over twenty-five years at TrueNorth Health Center, we have helped countless people restore and maintain their health. Our state-of-the-art facility serves only healthful foods. In addition, we provide medically supervised water-only and juice fasting, medical and chiropractic services, psychotherapy and counseling, and massage and bodywork. Our health-education programs show people how to adopt a health-promoting diet and lifestyle. The people we treat often see rapid reductions in high blood pressure and inflammation. Many are able to reduce or eliminate the use of prescription drugs; avoid invasive procedures, such as dialysis or surgery; and find relief from chronic and disabling diseases, including heart disease and autoimmune diseases. In large part, they achieve astounding results simply by changing their diets. They are proof positive that our personal health is predominantly determined by our dietary and lifestyle choices.

If you're ready to take the steps that will renew your health, then prepare to align your diet with nature's design. The recipes in this book provide the benefits of a plant-based, whole-foods diet that resembles what our ancient ancestors ate. Vegetables, fruits, beans, grains, nuts, seeds, and avocados are low in calorie density, which will help you to stay trim. They also are high in nutrient density, providing the many nutrients and micronutrients that are vital to health. Finally, they are low in harmful saturated fats and cholesterol, both of which are associated with a host of diseases. When you consume these whole, natural foods, you'll lose the tendency to overeat and will return rapidly to your optimal weight. No other diet can compare.

When you focus on *what* you eat and not on *how much*, you'll never have to count calories again. Enjoying the right foods in abundance will leave you feeling satisfied, not hungry or deprived. Before long, you'll grow accustomed to this new "normal." In fact, after just a few weeks of eating whole, natural foods, your taste buds will readapt. You'll remember what real food tastes like, and you'll love it.

Removing unhealthful foods from your diet leaves room for endless variety. You'll expand your dining repertoire and sample a host of plant-based foods that you may not have encountered before. For example, some recipes in this book incorporate the exotic tastes of jicama, kabocha squash, plantains, and sunchokes. But don't despair that you'll be leaving behind familiar favorites. Chef Bravo has given coleslaw, French toast, lasagne, onion soup, and even pizza a wholesome makeover.

How appropriate that "bravo" means a shout of approval. I applaud Chef Bravo for developing the delectable dishes that have brought renewed health to our participants at True-North Health Center. Now his recipes can do the same for you. In addition, I applaud you for your courage to change. Bravo!

Alan Goldhamer, DC, Director
TrueNorth Health Center
Santa Rosa, California
HealthPromoting.com

CHAPTER I

Getting Started

THE BEST CHEFS ARE NOT ALWAYS THE MOST TALENTED. Rather, they are organized and make things simple for themselves. The same is true of home cooks. Organized cooks everywhere are able to prepare wonderful dishes without turning the kitchen into a disaster area in the process. This section includes simple but valuable advice, especially if you want to find yourself more comfortable in your own kitchen.

Cooking at Home

Are you ready to dazzle your family and guests with great meals? Do you want to make them envious of how easy you make it look? Then follow these steps:

1. Start with a clean kitchen. Cooking in a dirty kitchen makes it hard to produce great dishes.

2. Keep your work area clean by quickly removing scraps and trash. When prepping fruits and vegetables, put a container for scraps (which you'll use to make vegetable broth) close to the cutting board where you are working. Use the back of your knife to push the scraps into the container as you work. Similarly, keep the trash can close and push trash into it.

3. Reuse pots and pans between washings. Cooking without oil makes it possible to use pots and pans multiple times without having to wash them. Simply empty the contents of a hot pot or pan and rinse it with water before it cools down. Swirl the water around long enough to remove any morsels that might be stuck.

4. Make a reusable grocery list. Categorize it by sections, such as fruits, vegetables, grains, and so on. Laminate the list and stick it on the refrigerator with a magnet. Using a dry erase marker, keep a running list of what's needed for the next shopping trip.

5. Recruit the kids. Children usually love to help with cooking. They can do simple tasks when they are little, and as they get older, they can help out more and more. The best part of having them help is that they (usually) work for free.

Equipment

A good cook builds up a useful supply of tools over time. Don't be discouraged by the long list of items suggested in this section. Start by using the tools and appliances you already have, then add to your collection as your skills and culinary repertoire grow.

Appliances

blender

citrus juicer

electric mixer

food processor

immersion blender

juicer (optional)

spice or coffee grinder

Pots and Pans

Because you'll be cooking in dry pots and pans without fat, you'll want the heaviest gauge cookware you can get. It can be expensive, but the value and longevity of high-quality cookware is worth the investment.

baking pans (including 9-inch round, 9-inch square, and 13 x 9-inch)

rimmed baking sheets, 2

saucepans with lids (small, medium, and large)

skillets (small, medium, and large)

soup pot (6-quart)

steamer basket insert

stockpot (12-quart)

Storage Containers

plastic containers (1-quart) with lids, 4

plastic containers (2-quart) with lids, 4 (including at least 2 square containers)

plastic containers (4-quart) with lids, 2

large storage container for stock

ziplock freezer bags, 1-quart and 1-gallon size

Tools

aluminum foil

chef's knife

cutting board

fine-mesh strainers,
    1 large and 1 small

flat rubber spatula

ice-cream scoop, 1 large

ladles, 1 large and 1 small

long serrated slicing knife

mallet

mandoline

measuring cups, dry
    (nesting metal or plastic)

measuring cups, wet (glass)

measuring spoons

melon baller

metal spatula

Microplane zester

mixing bowls,
    1 large and 2 medium

parchment paper

paring knife

pastry bags, 2

pastry brush

pastry tips,
    1 round and 1 star-shaped

plastic gloves

rolling pin

serving spoons, 2

sharpening steel

slotted serving spoons, 2

tongs

vegetable peelers, 1 straight
    and 1 Y-shaped

wire whisk

wooden spoons, 2

Two Weeks of Daily Menus
Day 1

Breakfast:

Raisin-Cinnamon Oatmeal (page 39)

Fresh fruit

Lunch: Mixed Sprouts and Kelp Noodle
Salad (page 64)

Creamy Sunchoke Soup with Watercress
(page 48)

Polenta Croutons (page 32)

Dinner:

Boulangère Potatoes (page 78) with
Roasted Bell Pepper Dressing (page 73)

Garbanzo Beans and Kale with Meyer Lemon
and Parsley Dressing (page 88)

Broccoli Slaw (page 61)

Total Calories	1,945	% of Calories
Carbohydrates (g)	370	74%
Protein (g)	62	10%
Fat (g)	37	16%
Micronutrients		**Daily Target**
Sodium (mg)	658	< 1,200
Potassium (mg)	7,152	> 4,700
Calcium (mg)	812	> 1,000
Omega-3 (g)	2.4	> 1.5

Day 2

Breakfast:

Baked Plantains with Coconut-Vanilla Granola
(page 42)

Fresh fruit

Lunch:

Hearts of Palm Salad (page 65)

Orange-Cinnamon Rice Pudding (page 125)

Dinner:

Red Lentil Loaf with Bell Pepper Coulis
(page 96)

Steamed vegetables with Tomato-Herb
Dressing (page 72)

Yellow Corn Chowder (page 54)

Total Calories	2,584	% of Calories
Carbohydrates (g)	503	74%
Protein (g)	84	10%
Fat (g)	45	16%
Micronutrients		**Daily Target**
Sodium (mg)	1,200	< 1,200
Potassium (mg)	11,670	> 4,700
Calcium (mg)	1,092	> 1,000
Omega-3 (g)	2.8	> 1.5

Day 3

Breakfast:
Breakfast Potatoes (page 44)
Fresh berries

Lunch:
Kabocha Squash and Yellow Curry Soup
     (page 49)
2 cups cooked forbidden rice
     (see page 25)
Steamed vegetables with Avocado-Corn
     Dressing (page 71)

Dinner:
Lasagne (page 104)
Grilled Ratatouille with Pesto Sauce (page 80)

Total Calories	2,273	% of Calories
Carbohydrates (g)	463	79%
Protein (g)	81	10%
Fat (g)	29	11%
Micronutrients		**Daily Target**
Sodium (mg)	1,370	< 1,200
Potassium (mg)	13,215	> 4,700
Calcium (mg)	1,202	> 1,000
Omega-3 (g)	3.1	> 1.5

Day 4

Breakfast:
Oatmeal "French Toast" (page 40)
     with Dried Peach Sauce (page 112)
Fresh fruit

Lunch:
Double Squash with Pecans and
     Dried Cherries (page 76)
Cannellini Bean Stew (page 92)

Dinner:
Bravo Pizza with Polenta Crust (page 110)
Yellow Split Pea Stew (page 94)

Total Calories	2,281	% of Calories
Carbohydrates (g)	480	81%
Protein (g)	73	10%
Fat (g)	24	9%
Micronutrients		**Daily Target**
Sodium (mg)	501	< 1,200
Potassium (mg)	9,194	> 4,700
Calcium (mg)	803	> 1,000
Omega-3 (g)	2.3	> 1.5

Day 5

Breakfast:

Banana-Kale Smoothie (page 38)

Lunch:

Cream of Asparagus Soup (page 46)

Oven-Roasted Tomatoes with Arugula
    (page 79)

Black Bean Stew (page 98)

Dinner:

Quinoa Salad (page 89)

Steamed vegetables with Apple-Mustard
    Dressing (page 69)

Mango-Banana Pie (page 129)

Total Calories	2,121	% of Calories
Carbohydrates (g)	372	66%
Protein (g)	74	11%
Fat (g)	54	23%
Micronutrients		**Daily Target**
Sodium (mg)	1,479	< 1,200
Potassium (mg)	10,137	> 4,700
Calcium (mg)	1,180	> 1,000
Omega-3 (g)	3.1	> 1.5

Day 6

Breakfast:

Scrambled Tofu and Curried Potatoes
    (page 43)

Fresh apples

Lunch:

Sea Vegetable and Baked Rice Soup
    (page 55)

Hawaiian Salad (page 64)

Dinner:

Forbidden Rice and Garbanzo Patties
    with Tomatillo Salsa (page 100)

Sautéed Kale and Mushrooms
    with Ginger (page 77)

Total Calories	1,904	% of Calories
Carbohydrates (g)	344	68%
Protein (g)	79	13%
Fat (g)	40	19%
Micronutrients		**Daily Target**
Sodium (mg)	918	< 1,200
Potassium (mg)	7,884	> 4,700
Calcium (mg)	1,221	> 1,000
Omega-3 (g)	2.7	> 1.5

Day 7

Breakfast:

Banana-Pecan Bars (page 41)

Fresh fruit

Lunch:

Tortilla Soup (page 56) and Mustard-Braised
    Brussels Sprouts and Corn (page 82)

Dinner:

Black Bean Tamale Pie (page 106)

Chayote-Apple Slaw (page 60)

Total Calories	1,814	% of Calories
Carbohydrates (g)	322	66%
Protein (g)	48	8%
Fat (g)	53	26%
Micronutrients		**Daily Target**
Sodium (mg)	399	< 1,200
Potassium (mg)	5,610	> 4,700
Calcium (mg)	589	> 1,000
Omega-3 (g)	2.5	> 1.5

Day 8

Breakfast:

Mango-Papaya Smoothie (page 38)

Lunch:

Twice-Baked Yams and Mashed Potatoes
    (page 81)

Creamy Cauliflower Soup (page 47)

Dinner:

Bravo Chili (page 90)

Steamed vegetables

Fig-Pecan Bars (page 126)

Total Calories	2,311	% of Calories
Carbohydrates (g)	427	71%
Protein (g)	83	11%
Fat (g)	47	18%
Micronutrients		**Daily Target**
Sodium (mg)	1,943	< 1,200
Potassium (mg)	12,150	> 4,700
Calcium (mg)	1,319	> 1,000
Omega-3 (g)	2.7	> 1.5

Day 9

Breakfast:

Pineapple-Coconut Oatmeal (page 39)

Fresh fruit

Lunch:

Toasted Barley and Tomato Stew (page 95)

Raw vegetable sticks with Flaxseed Dressing
    (page 74)

Steamed vegetables

Dinner:

Roasted Eggplant and Heirloom Tomatoes
    (page 85)

Brown Lentil Stew (page 93)

Apple-Strawberry Gelée (page 124)

Total Calories	1,889	% of Calories
Carbohydrates (g)	376	76%
Protein (g)	66	12%
Fat (g)	26	12%
Micronutrients		**Daily Target**
Sodium (mg)	1,284	< 1,200
Potassium (mg)	8,284	> 4,700
Calcium (mg)	779	> 1,000
Omega-3 (g)	3.1	> 1.5

Day 10

Breakfast:

Oatmeal "French Toast" (page 40)
    with Dried Peach Sauce (page 112)

Fresh fruit

Lunch:

Potato Wedge Salad (page 83)

Baked Tofu Stir-Fry with Sweet-and-Sour
    Sauce (page 108)

Dinner:

Blue Cornmeal Loaf (page 97)

Mucha Onion Soup (page 51)

Steamed vegetables

Total Calories	2,540	% of Calories
Carbohydrates (g)	536	81%
Protein (g)	83	10%
Fat (g)	26	9%
Micronutrients		**Daily Target**
Sodium (mg)	1,191	< 1,200
Potassium (mg)	10,217	> 4,700
Calcium (mg)	880	> 1,000
Omega-3 (g)	2.4	> 1.5

Day 11

Breakfast:

Coconut-Vanilla Granola (page 36)

Fresh fruit

Lunch:

Wild Mushroom Soup (page 52)

Beet and Citrus Salad (page 59)

Dinner:

Eggplant Cannelloni with Bravo
    Tomato Sauce (page 102)

Raw vegetable sticks with
    Pineapple-Tarragon Dressing (page 68)

Apple-Pecan Cobbler (page 128)

Total Calories	2,309	% of Calories
Carbohydrates (g)	459	75%
Protein (g)	58	8%
Fat (g)	43	17%
Micronutrients		**Daily Target**
Sodium (mg)	482	< 1,200
Potassium (mg)	7,339	> 4,700
Calcium (mg)	686	> 1,000
Omega-3 (g)	2.2	> 1.5

Day 12

Breakfast:

Breakfast Potatoes (page 44)

Fresh fruit

Lunch:

Potato-Leek Soup (page 50)

Quinoa Salad (page 89)

Steamed vegetables

Dinner:

Tofu and Tempeh Skewers with Roasted
    Garlic and Tamarind Glaze (page 109)

Pickled Vegetable Slaw (page 63)

Sweet Yam Pie (page 130)

Total Calories	2,268	% of Calories
Carbohydrates (g)	445	76%
Protein (g)	80	11%
Fat (g)	33	13%
Micronutrients		**Daily Target**
Sodium (mg)	1,298	< 1,200
Potassium (mg)	10,900	> 4,700
Calcium (mg)	1,058	> 1,000
Omega-3 (g)	2.7	> 1.5

Day 13

Breakfast:

Apple-Cherry Oatmeal (page 39)

Fresh fruit

Lunch:

Veggie Wraps with Herbed Hummus
    (page 84)

Fresh Herb and Strawberry Salad (page 58)

2 cups cooked Bhutanese red rice

Dinner:

Butternut Squash and Corn Tamales
    (page 107)

Celery Root Slaw (page 62)

Total Calories	2,754	% of Calories
Carbohydrates (g)	494	69%
Protein (g)	66	7%
Fat (g)	75	24%
Micronutrients		**Daily Target**
Sodium (mg)	527	< 1,200
Potassium (mg)	6,994	> 4,700
Calcium (mg)	1,064	> 1,000
Omega-3 (g)	3.9	> 1.5

Day 14

Breakfast:

Banana-Pecan Bars (page 41)

Fresh fruit

Lunch:

Bravo Coleslaw (page 60)

Kabocha Squash and Yellow Curry Soup
    (page 49)

Dinner:

Bravo Pizza with Polenta Crust (page 110)

Raw green salad with Blood Orange
    Dressing (page 69)

Peach-Blueberry Crisp (page 127)

Total Calories	2,091	% of Calories
Carbohydrates (g)	374	66%
Protein (g)	46	7%
Fat (g)	63	27%
Micronutrients		**Daily Target**
Sodium (mg)	446	< 1,200
Potassium (mg)	7,140	> 4,700
Calcium (mg)	576	> 1,000
Omega-3 (g)	2.5	> 1.5

Breakfast Potatoes, p. 44

Mango-Papaya Smoothie, p. 38

Recipes

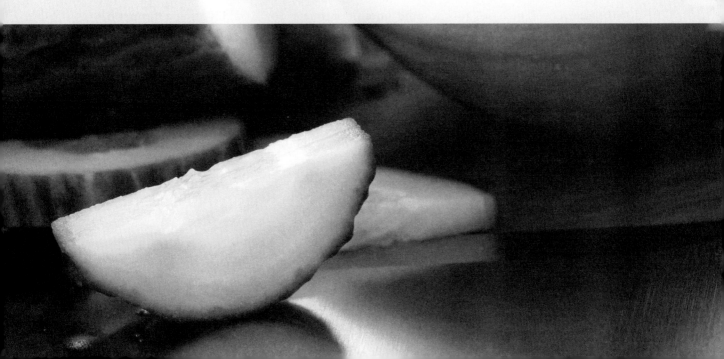

CHAPTER 2
The Basics

THIS CHAPTER CONTAINS A NUMBER OF FUNDAMENTAL TECHNIQUES AND RECIPES that you will need to create the great dishes in this book. Mastering these basics is essential for preparing healthful meals. As you get accustomed to using them, you can incorporate these techniques and recipes into a wider variety of dishes that suit your preferences and those of your family and friends.

Steaming Vegetables

It can be difficult to get steamed vegetables to turn out perfect every time. Often, at a friend's house—or even a restaurant—I am served vegetables that are either too hard to chew or too soft and dull in color. Many of the sample menus in chapter 1 (pages 14 to 20) include steamed vegetables.

Wash and trim the vegetables, then cut them according to the recipe instructions. If you'll be steaming different vegetables at the same time, group them into the following categories: leafy vegetables (such as cabbage, kale, and swiss chard), soft vegetables (such as asparagus, broccoli, celery, and zucchini), and hard vegetables (such as carrots, rutabagas, and turnips). Leafy vegetables should be cut into 2-inch pieces. Soft and hard vegetables should be bite-sized and sliced about $\frac{1}{4}$ inch thick.

Put $\frac{1}{2}$ inch of water in a pot with a steamer basket. (The size of the pot will depend on the quantity of vegetables being steamed.) Cover and bring to a boil over high heat. Once the water comes to a rapid boil and a plentiful amount of steam is escaping from the pot, uncover the pot, put the vegetables in the steamer basket, and cover the pot. If you are steaming vegetables with different densities, put the hard vegetables in first, add the soft vegetables 45 seconds later, add the leafy vegetables 45 seconds after that, and cook 60 seconds longer. If you are steaming one type of vegetable or vegetables with the same density, cook hard vegetables for $2\frac{1}{2}$ minutes, soft vegetables for $1\frac{3}{4}$ minutes, and leafy vegetables for 1 minute.

If a steamer basket is not available, don't panic. (I actually prefer steaming vegetables without a basket). Put $\frac{1}{8}$ inch of water in a pot. Put the vegetables in the pot in the same order noted earlier, cover, and cook for the same amount of time as you would if using a steamer basket. Lift and shake the pot back and forth a few times while the vegetables are cooking so they will cook more evenly.

Note: Very hard vegetables, such as beets and potatoes, cannot be steamed without a steamer basket. When steaming beets and potatoes, put 2 to 3 inches of water in the pot and cook, covered, for 30 to 40 minutes. Keep an eye on the water level and add more water if needed. If the water evaporates, the bottom of the pot will burn and ruin the flavor of the vegetables.

Cooking Rice

In this book you'll find recipes that call for either brown or forbidden rice. For every cup of rice, use 2 cups of vegetable broth (preferably homemade, page 28). Put the rice and broth in a saucepan and bring to a rapid boil over high heat. (The size of the saucepan will depend on the quantity of rice being cooked.) Decrease the heat to low, cover, and cook for 30 to 35 minutes.

Cooking in Dry Pots and Pans

In chapter 1, I recommend that you buy the heaviest gauge cookware you can afford because you'll be cooking in dry pots and pans. Many recipes in this book call for dry cooking vegetables, and sometimes even fruits. This healthful technique requires no oil. The instructions for dry cooking vary in each recipe. Stir as instructed and allow the pot or pan and its contents to brown as instructed. For easier cleanup, immediately rinse or wash pans after dry cooking.

Preparing Dried Legumes for Cooking

Spread the dried beans, lentils, or peas on a rimmed baking sheet and remove any stones or other debris. Transfer to a large strainer or colander and rinse thoroughly under cold running water. Soak the beans, lentils, or peas as instructed for each recipe (not all recipes require soaking). Put the legumes in a large bowl or pot and add cold water until it covers them by at least 2 inches. Let soak at room temperature or in the refrigerator for 8 to 12 hours. Some recipes specify that legumes be soaked in vegetable broth. In these cases, the soaking liquid is retained and used in the recipe.

Roasting Garlic

Preheat the oven to 350 degrees F. Arrange peeled garlic cloves on a rimmed baking sheet in a single layer. Roast until golden brown, 12 to 15 minutes. Stored in a sealed container in the refrigerator, roasted garlic will keep for 2 weeks.

Roasting Peppers

Preheat the oven to 350 degrees F. Line a rimmed baking sheet with parchment paper. Slice the peppers lengthwise and remove the seeds and stems. Arrange the peppers skin-side up on the lined baking sheet. Roast until the skins start to turn black, about 20 minutes. Transfer the peppers to a bowl, cover with plastic wrap, and let rest for 10 minutes to loosen the skins. Peel off the skins with your fingers. Stored in a sealed container in the refrigerator, roasted peppers will keep for 1 week.

Toasting Nuts and Seeds

Preheat the oven to 350 degrees F. Spread the nuts or seeds on a rimmed baking sheet in a single layer. Bake for 3 to 5 minutes.

Raw or Toasted Nuts and Seeds?

Which is better: raw or toasted nuts and seeds? This is a question that many TrueNorth guests have asked me. My answer depends on what works best for each person.

The style of cooking advocated at TrueNorth and described in this book is designed for optimal health. To that end, I recommend raw nuts and seeds, which have greater nutritional value. However, this diet is also restrictive, so I look for ways to make the food as flavorful as possible. One way to do that is to use toasted nuts and seeds, which I prefer. My reasoning is that people may return to bad habits if they find their food bland, and they may be more likely to stay with the program if it is more flavorful.

Blanching Herbs

Blanching herbs preserves their bright colors and fresh flavors. To blanch herbs, fill a saucepan with water and bring to a boil over high heat. (The size of the saucepan will depend on the quantity of herbs being blanched.) Prepare the herbs by picking the leaves off the stems. Put a container of ice water next to the boiling water. Drop the herbs in the boiling water for 3 to 5 seconds, stirring once. Using a wire strainer, pull the herbs out of the boiling water and immediately plunge them into the ice water. After 30 seconds, remove the herbs from the ice water and dry them with paper towels. Stored in a covered container in the refrigerator, blanched herbs will keep for about 3 days. **Note:** It is especially important to blanch fresh tarragon before using.

Juicing Fruits and Vegetables without a Juicer

Cut the fruits or vegetables to be juiced into 1-inch pieces. Put them in a blender and add $1/3$ cup of water per for each cup of diced fruits or vegetables. Process on high speed for about 1 minute. Strain through a fine-mesh strainer.

Cutting Corn Kernels from the Cob

Shuck the corn. Stand one cob at a time in the center of a 2-quart container. Holding the upper tip of the cob, use a sharp paring knife to slice downward from the top of the cob. The kernels will fall into the container. Rotate the cob and repeat until all the kernels have been cut off.

Cleaning and Using Leeks

It is very important to remove all dirt from leeks, which seem to collect much more than you can see. Trim off the root ends and tough green parts of the leaves, and use only the tender white and light green parts of the leeks in recipes. Cut the leeks as needed for the recipe and put them in a strainer. Rinse thoroughly under running water for 30 to 40 seconds, making sure that all surfaces of the leeks are rinsed well and no dirt or grit remains between the layers.

Vegetable Broth

VEGETABLE BROTH IS THE FOUNDATION OF THIS BOOK *and is used in most bean, lentil, polenta, rice, soup, and stew recipes, and even in some salad dressings. It is the best tool I can give you as you transition to a diet free from added salt. This recipe produces a very flavorful broth and can be made with just about any vegetable trimmings (see notes, next page). As you prepare vegetables for meals, simply save the cores, peelings, stems, tops and bottoms, and other trimmings to use as broth ingredients.*

Cores from bell peppers, cabbages, cauliflower, corn, tomatoes, and other vegetables

Peelings from asparagus, carrots, celery root, ginger, kohlrabi, rutabagas, sunchokes, turnips, and other vegetables

Stems from broccoli, collard greens, green beans, herbs, kale, mushrooms, Swiss chard, watercress, and other vegetables

Tops and bottoms from carrots, celery, green beans, leeks, onions, zucchini, and other vegetables

Trimmings from bell peppers, cabbages, carrots, fennel, garlic, onions, peas, and other vegetables

Save and refrigerate items from the above list for up to 3 days. Rinse thoroughly and discard anything you can't properly clean. Put the ingredients in a pot. Add water until it covers the ingredients by 1 to 2 inches. Bring to a boil over high heat. Decrease the heat to medium and simmer for 30 minutes. Pour the broth through a fine-mesh strainer before using.

Stored in a sealed container, Vegetable Broth will keep for 7 to 10 days in the refrigerator and 6 months in the freezer. (Let the broth cool to room temperature before refrigerating or freezing it.)

NOTES

- Not all of the above ingredients are edible, but they are full of flavor. Save them and use them according to your preferences. The few items I don't use are artichoke and eggplant trimmings and the outer layers of onions, which all tend to make a bitter-flavored stock.

- For additional flavor, try adding bay leaves, celery seeds, coriander seeds, cumin seeds, fennel seeds, and peppercorns.

- There are a number of incentives for making broth at home (besides great taste). For example, it's economical. Every quart of vegetable broth you buy at the store costs a few dollars, but homemade broth is made from scraps you would otherwise discard or compost. In addition, it won't have any unnatural flavorings or additives.

- Frozen broth frequently comes in handy. If you cook for two people, freeze the broth in pint containers. If you cook for four people, freeze the broth in quart containers. If you often need just a small amount of broth to steam-fry vegetables, freeze some broth in ice-cube trays and pop out a cube whenever you need one.

- If you are not sure whether making broth is worthwhile, make a pot of this wonderful broth and drink a cup of it while it is still hot, just as if it were a hot cup of tea. Then ask yourself whether you want to cook rice or make other recipes with plain water or flavorful homemade broth.

Asian Broth

MOST ASIAN MARKETS SELL FRESH GALANGAL AND KAFFIR LIME LEAVES, *which give this recipe exceptional flavor and flair. Asian Broth is used in Kabocha Squash and Yellow Curry Soup (page 49) and Sea Vegetable and Baked Rice Soup (page 55).*

I pound fresh ginger, cut into I-inch pieces

I pound fresh lemongrass, cut into I-inch pieces

½ pound fresh galangal, cut into I-inch pieces

6 stalks celery, cut into I-inch pieces

3 yellow onions, peeled and cut into I-inch pieces

3 tomatoes, cut into I-inch pieces

3 carrots, scrubbed and cut into I-inch pieces

I head garlic, halved

5 kaffir lime leaves

Put all the ingredients in a large soup pot. Add water until it covers the ingredients by about 2 inches. Bring to a boil over high heat. Cover, decrease the heat to low, and simmer for 30 minutes. Pour the broth through a fine-mesh strainer before using.

Stored in a sealed container, Asian Broth will keep for 7 to 10 days in the refrigerator and 6 months in the freezer.

NOTE: Vegetable broth (preferably homemade, page 28) can be used instead of water when a stronger flavor is desired.

Cooked Garbanzo Beans

COOKED GARBANZO BEANS ARE GREAT TO HAVE AROUND. *They can be used to enhance entrées, salads, stews, and vegetable dishes, making them an essential ingredient in a vegan kitchen.*

3 cups dried garbanzo beans (see page 31), soaked in water for 8 to 12 hours

8 quarts vegetable broth (preferably homemade, page 28)

1 tablespoon granulated garlic

1 tablespoon granulated onion

Drain the beans and put them in a large pot along with the broth. Bring to a simmer (not a boil) over medium heat and cook uncovered, stirring occasionally, until very soft, 1½ to 3 hours. Frequently use a ladle to skim off any foam that forms at the surface. Discard the foam.

Stir in the granulated garlic and granulated onion. Cover, decrease the heat to low, and cook for 30 minutes longer. The beans should be so tender that they seem overcooked. They will firm up a bit when they cool. Stored in a sealed container in the refrigerator, Cooked Garbanzo Beans will keep for 5 to 7 days.

NOTE: The broth from the cooked garbanzo beans is extremely flavorful, so don't discard it. Whenever I have some, I use it to cook polenta or soup.

Per serving (1 cup): calories: 218.4, protein: 11.6 g, carbohydrates: 36.4 g, fat: 3.6 g, calcium: 63 mg, sodium: 174.4 mg, omega-3: 0.1 g

Polenta Crusts or Croutons

YIELD: 4 (9-INCH) PIZZA CRUSTS, OR ABOUT 8 CUPS OF CROUTONS

HERE, THE POLENTA IS COOKED, COOLED, AND CHILLED *in the refrigerator until it is firm enough to be cut into various shapes with a knife. Use this recipe to make wholesome, gluten-free pizza crusts or croutons for floating on soups or dressing up salads.*

8 cups vegetable broth (preferably homemade, page 28)

2 cups yellow corn grits

2 tablespoons diced shallot

**1 tablespoon chopped fresh basil, or
1 teaspoon dried**

**1 tablespoon chopped fresh parsley, or
1 teaspoon dried**

**1 tablespoon blanched fresh tarragon (see page 26), chopped, or
1 teaspoon dried**

**1 tablespoon chopped fresh thyme, or
1 teaspoon dried**

1 teaspoon salt-free seasoning blend

Put the broth in a large saucepan over high heat and bring to a boil. Whisk the corn grits into the broth and continue whisking vigorously for 1 minute. Decrease the heat to low and cook for 20 minutes, whisking about once per minute. Stir in the shallot, basil, parsley, tarragon, thyme, and salt-free seasoning blend and remove from the heat.

To prep the polenta for making pizza crusts, pour the hot polenta into a 9-inch round pan; the polenta should be about 2 inches deep. Let cool at room temperature for 20 to 25 minutes, then refrigerate uncovered for 8 to 10 hours, until firm. Once firm, cover loosely with plastic wrap.

When you're ready to make the pizza crusts, turn the polenta out onto a cutting board. Use a long, sharp, and preferably serrated knife to carefully slice the polenta horizontally (use a sawing motion) into four rounds, each about 1/2 inch thick. (For instructions on how to bake and use the crusts, see Bravo Pizza with Polenta Crust, page 110.)

To prep the polenta for making croutons, pour the hot polenta into a 13 x 9-inch baking pan. Let cool at room temperature for 20 to 25 minutes, then refrigerate uncovered for 8 to 10 hours, until firm. Once firm, cover loosely with plastic wrap.

When you're ready to make the croutons, preheat the oven to 350 degrees F. Line a rimmed baking sheet with parchment paper.

Turn the polenta out onto a cutting board and cut it into ½-inch cubes. Arrange on the lined baking sheet and bake for 20 to 25 minutes, stirring once or twice, until golden brown and crispy all over.

NOTE: Once poured into the pan for either crust or croutons, polenta can be covered and stored in the refrigerator, where it will keep for 5 days. Freezing is not recommended.

Per serving (1 crust or 2 cups croutons): calories: 220.8, protein: 5 g, carbohydrates: 46.9 g, fat: 2.2 g, calcium: 3.7 mg, sodium: 121.4 mg, omega-3: 0 g

VARIATIONS

- For added flavor, stir ½ cup of finely diced cooked vegetables, such as roasted mushrooms or tomatoes, into the polenta before pouring into the pan.
- To use as an alternative to toast or breadsticks, preheat the oven to 350 degrees F. Cut the polenta into squares or strips. Line a baking sheet with parchment paper and arrange the pieces in a single layer. Bake for 20 to 25 minutes, until golden and crisp.

Tamale Dough

MASA HARINA, A TYPE OF FINELY GROUND CORN FLOUR *used in traditional Mexican cooking, can be purchased at any Latin market. If you find two varieties, choose the regular kind (which is what I prefer) over the type that is specifically intended for making tamales. Tamale Dough is used in Black Bean Tamale Pie (page 106) and Butternut Squash and Corn Tamales (page 107).*

9 cups vegetable broth (preferably homemade, page 28)

1 teaspoon granulated garlic

1 teaspoon granulated onion

¾ cup sunflower seeds, soaked in cold water for 3 hours

4 cups masa harina

2 ½ teaspoons baking powder

¾ cup raw tahini

Put the broth, granulated garlic, and granulated onion in a medium saucepan and bring to a simmer over medium-high heat. Simmer until the liquid is reduced by half, about 15 minutes. Let cool until lukewarm.

Drain the sunflower seeds, saving about ½ cup of the soaking water. Put the seeds in a food processor and process into a smooth paste, adding the soaking water, 1 tablespoon at a time, as needed. (All the soaking water may not be needed.)

Put the masa harina and baking powder in a large bowl. Using an electric mixer, mix on low speed for 30 seconds. Add the broth mixture and continue mixing on low speed until thoroughly combined. Increase the mixer speed to medium and mix for 5 minutes. Add the sunflower seed paste and tahini and mix on medium speed until all the ingredients are well combined. Increase the mixer speed to high and mix for 5 minutes. Stored in a sealed container in the refrigerator, Tamale Dough will keep for 3 days.

NOTES

- To avoid splashing, cover the mixing bowl with plastic wrap before increasing the mixer speed.

- A hand mixer is not recommended for this recipe, as the tamale dough is too thick for that piece of equipment.

Per serving (½ cup): calories: 219.8, protein: 6.4 g, carbohydrates: 27.7 g, fat: 10.5 g, calcium: 98.5 mg, sodium: 40.9 mg, omega-3: 0.1 g

Nutty Dough

NUTTY DOUGH BAKES INTO A CRUNCHY, FLAKY CRUST. *This recipe makes top and bottom crusts for Fig-Pecan Bars (page 126) or top crusts for a double batch of Peach-Blueberry Crisp (page 127).*

3 cups oat flour

½ cup ground almonds

½ cup unsweetened shredded dried coconut

½ cup ground pecans

1 teaspoon baking powder

1 cup unsweetened pineapple juice

½ cup unsweetened applesauce

2 tablespoons almond butter

Put the oat flour, almonds, coconut, pecans, and baking powder in a large bowl and stir with a wooden spoon until well combined. Put the pineapple juice, applesauce, and almond butter in a small bowl and whisk until well blended. Pour the pineapple juice mixture into the oat flour mixture. Stir with a wooden spoon for 1 minute to form the dough.

NOTE: The dough will be very soft at first. The flour will absorb the moisture as you work with it. Ideally, this dough should be used right after it's made. If allowed to sit too long, it becomes stiff and difficult to work with.

Per serving (½ cup): calories: 362, protein: 8.4 g, carbohydrates: 31.2 g, fat: 23.9 g, calcium: 40.7 mg, sodium: 9.2 mg, omega-3: 0.1 g

VARIATION: For a more pronounced flavor, use 1 cup of either almonds or pecans and omit the other.

Coconut-Vanilla Granola

YIELD: 10 CUPS

WHEN COCONUT-VANILLA GRANOLA IS IN THE OVEN, *the house smells like a bakery.*

2 cups unsweetened apple juice

2 cups unsweetened pineapple juice

¼ cup coarsely chopped dried peaches

¼ teaspoon ground cinnamon

¼ teaspoon ground nutmeg

1 vanilla bean, split lengthwise, or 1 teaspoon alcohol-free vanilla extract

10 cups old-fashioned or quick-cooking rolled oats

1½ cups unsweetened shredded dried coconut

Put the apple juice, pineapple juice, peaches, cinnamon, nutmeg, and vanilla bean in a medium saucepan and stir to combine. Bring to a simmer over low heat, cover, and simmer for 15 minutes, or until the peaches are plump and the amount of liquid is slightly reduced. Remove from the heat.

Carefully remove the vanilla bean, scrape the seeds back into the saucepan, and discard the bean. Let cool for about 10 minutes, then transfer to a blender. Process on high speed until smooth. Transfer to a large bowl and let cool to room temperature.

While the peach mixture is cooling, preheat the oven to 250 degrees F. Line a rimmed baking sheet with parchment paper.

Add the oats and coconut to the peach mixture and stir with a wooden spoon until thoroughly combined. Spread the mixture on the lined baking sheet. Bake until the granola is golden brown, about 1½ hours, stirring about every 20 minutes with the wooden spoon to break up any large clumps.

Remove from the oven and cool to room temperature. Transfer to an airtight container. Stored in a cool, dry place, Coconut-Vanilla Granola will keep for 1 month.

Per serving (1 cup): calories: 459.9, protein: 12 g, carbohydrates: 72.8 g, fat: 14.6 g, calcium: 57.5 mg, sodium: 13.4 mg, omega-3: 0.1 g

CHAPTER 3

Breakfast

BREAKFAST IS A VERY IMPORTANT MEAL, SO WHY NOT START YOUR DAY OFF WITH THE VERY BEST? This chapter offers a range of delectable tastes and textures that are guaranteed to please. Whether you like to eat and run or slowly savor your morning meal, you'll find options here that will fit into your routine.

Fruit is the original fast food. A breakfast of fresh fruit makes an extremely quick and nutritious meal. Another convenient option is the breakfast smoothie, which can be made from endless combinations of fruits, vegetables, nuts, and seeds. Smoothies made from these natural foods provide a rich complement of nutrients and micronutrients.

A few of these recipes take a little more time to prepare, and they are perfect for leisurely weekend breakfasts. However, some preparation can be started the night before, so with a little planning and preparation, you can make these breakfasts any day of the week.

Banana-Kale Smoothie

YIELD: 1 SERVING

THE FIRST TIME I TRIED THIS RECIPE, *I thought the kale would overpower the other ingredients and give the smoothie a bitter taste. That's not how it turned out, however. This smoothie has a sweet and pleasant flavor.*

1 cup unsweetened pineapple juice

1 ripe banana

1 kale leaf, stemmed

½ cup cubed celery

½ cup ice (optional)

¼ cup old-fashioned or quick-cooking rolled oats

6 or 7 pecans, toasted (see page 26)

Put all the ingredients in a blender and process on high speed until smooth. Pour into a tall glass. Serve immediately.

NOTE: For a thicker smoothie, add more pecans.

Per serving: calories: 530.4, protein: 10.9 g, carbohydrates: 90.8 g, fat: 17.3 g, calcium: 267.8 mg, sodium: 244.9 mg, omega-3: 0.4 g

Mango-Papaya Smoothie

SEE PHOTO FACING PAGE 21   YIELD: 1 SERVING

THE TROPICAL FLAVOR OF THIS SMOOTHIE *reminds me of a white sandy beach on a sunny day. What a great way to start the day!*

1 mango, diced

1 cup diced papaya

1 cup fresh spinach, lightly packed

½ cup cubed celery

½ cup ice (optional)

¼ cup old-fashioned or quick-cooking rolled oats

6 or 7 cashews

1 tablespoon chopped fresh ginger

Put all the ingredients in a blender and process on high speed until smooth. Pour into a tall glass. Serve immediately.

NOTE: For a thicker smoothie, add more cashews.

Per serving: calories: 391.2 protein: 9.7 g, carbohydrates: 75.6 g, fat: 8.8 g, calcium: 202.1 mg, sodium: 239.7 mg, omega-3: 0.2 g

Raisin-Cinnamon Oatmeal

YIELD: 6 SERVINGS

THIS DELICIOUS BREAKFAST IS QUICK AND EASY TO MAKE *and provides all of the heart-healthy benefits of oats without any of the artificial ingredients or sugar found in refined cereals. I suggest a few flavorful variations, but it's easy to create your own.*

8 cups unsweetened apple juice

Grated zest and juice of I orange

½ cup raisins

I teaspoon ground cinnamon

½ teaspoon ground nutmeg

4 cups quick-cooking rolled oats (not instant)

Put the apple juice, orange zest and juice, raisins, cinnamon, and nutmeg in a large saucepan and stir to combine. Bring to a boil over high heat. Add the oats and stir rapidly for 30 seconds. Cover, decrease the heat to low, and cook for 5 minutes. Serve hot.

Per serving: calories: 405, protein: 8 g, carbohydrates: 86.5 g, fat: 4.1 g, calcium: 74 mg, sodium: 17.9 mg, omega-3: 0.1 g

APPLE-CHERRY OATMEAL: Replace the orange zest and juice with 3 apples, peeled, cored, and diced, and the raisins with ½ cup of dried cherries.

Per serving: calories: 424.2, protein: 8.1 g, carbohydrates: 91.5 g, fat: 4.1 g, calcium: 64.5 mg, sodium: 16.5 mg, omega-3: 0.1 g

PINEAPPLE-COCONUT OATMEAL: Replace the apple juice with 8 cups of unsweetened pineapple juice, and replace the raisins with 2 cups of unsweetened shredded dried coconut.

Per serving: calories: 546.7, protein: 9.4 g, carbohydrates: 96.8 g, fat: 14.9 g, calcium: 84.8 mg, sodium: 91.1 mg, omega-3: 0.1 g

Oatmeal "French Toast"

YIELD: 4 SERVINGS

THESE TASTY TREATS CAN BE MADE IN ANY SHAPE YOU LIKE, *such as circles, squares, or triangles. Use cookie cutters in fancy shapes to celebrate holidays and other special occasions. I recommend cooking and chilling the oatmeal the night before you want to serve Oatmeal "French Toast."*

4 cups unsweetened apple juice

Grated zest and juice of 1 orange

½ cup raisins

1 teaspoon ground cinnamon

½ teaspoon ground nutmeg

3 cups quick-cooking rolled oats (not instant)

1 cup Dried Peach Sauce (page 112), warmed

Put the apple juice, orange zest and juice, raisins, cinnamon, and nutmeg in a medium saucepan and stir to combine. Bring to a boil over high heat. Add the oats and stir rapidly for 30 seconds. Cover, decrease the heat to low, and cook for 5 minutes.

Remove from the heat and uncover. Let the oatmeal cool for 10 minutes. Transfer to a 2-quart square container. Press down on the oatmeal with a spatula to remove all the air pockets and smooth the top. Once the oatmeal is cool to the touch, cover the container and refrigerate for 8 to 10 hours, until firm. At this stage, the oatmeal will keep for 1 week in the refrigerator.

When you're ready to make the Oatmeal "French Toast," preheat the oven to 350 degrees F. Line a rimmed baking sheet with parchment paper.

Uncover the oatmeal container, turn it upside down on a cutting board, and pop out the oatmeal. Cut it into thin slices, between ¼ and ½ inch thick. Put the slices on the lined baking sheet and bake for about 20 minutes, until golden brown.

Put the slices on serving plates and drizzle with the Dried Peach Sauce. Serve hot.

Per serving: calories: 453.6, protein: 9.4 g, carbohydrates: 97.3 g, fat: 4.5g, calcium: 79.5 mg, sodium: 18 mg, omega-3: 0.1 g

VARIATIONS

• Replace the apple juice with other juices, such as unsweetened pineapple or mango juice.

• Replace the raisins with other dried fruits, such as chopped apricots, cherries, or currants.

Banana-Pecan Bars

YIELD: 4 SERVINGS

STEEL-CUT OATS, WHICH ARE DENSER AND TAKE LONGER TO COOK THAN ROLLED OATS, *give these bars a hearty, chewy texture. I recommend cooking and chilling the oatmeal the night before you want to make Banana-Pecan Bars for breakfast.*

Bars

4 cups unsweetened apple juice

¼ cup raisins

1 teaspoon ground cinnamon

½ teaspoon ground nutmeg

1½ cups steel-cut oats

1 cup pecans, toasted (see page 26) and chopped

Sauce

1 cup unsweetened pineapple juice

1 teaspoon almond butter

4 ripe bananas, sliced into ¼-inch-thick rounds

To prep the bars, put the apple juice, raisins, cinnamon, and nutmeg in a medium saucepan and stir to combine. Bring to a boil over high heat. Add the oats and stir rapidly for 30 seconds. Decrease the heat to low and cook, stirring occasionally, for 30 minutes, or until the oats are tender.

Remove from the heat. Stir in the pecans and let cool for 10 minutes. Transfer to a 2-quart square container. Press down on the oatmeal with a spatula to remove all the air pockets and smooth the top. Once the oatmeal is cool to the touch, cover the container and refrigerate for 8 to 10 hours, until firm. At this stage, the oatmeal will keep for 1 week in the refrigerator.

When you're ready to make the Banana-Pecan Bars, preheat the oven to 350 degrees F. Line a rimmed baking sheet with parchment paper.

Uncover the oatmeal container, turn it upside down on a cutting board, and pop out the oatmeal. Cut the oatmeal into 1 x 5-inch strips and put them on the lined baking sheet. Bake for 20 minutes, until golden brown.

While the bars are baking, make the sauce. Put the pineapple juice and almond butter in a small saucepan and stir to combine. Bring to a boil over medium heat. Stir in the bananas. Decrease the heat to low and cook until the bananas are heated through, about 3 minutes.

Put the bars on serving plates and pour the warm sauce over the bars. Serve hot.

Per serving: 527.3 calories, protein: 7.8 g, carbohydrates: 86.8 g, fat: 19.7 g, calcium: 69 mg, sodium: 14.1 mg, omega-3: 0.3 g

Baked Plantains with Coconut-Vanilla Granola

YIELD: 4 SERVINGS

THIS SWEET BREAKFAST DISH CAN ALSO BE SERVED AS A DESSERT. *Use ripe plantains, which should be about half yellow and half speckled dark brown.*

4 ripe plantains, unpeeled

1 cup diced fresh or canned pineapple packed in juice, drained

1 cup unsweetened pineapple juice

½ vanilla bean, split lengthwise, or ½ teaspoon alcohol-free vanilla extract

2 cups Coconut-Vanilla Granola (page 36)

Preheat the oven to 400 degrees F. Line a rimmed baking sheet with parchment paper.

Put the plantains on the lined baking sheet and bake for 10 to 12 minutes, until the skins start to burst open.

Meanwhile, heat a small skillet over medium-high heat for 2 minutes. Put the pineapple in the hot skillet and cook, stirring frequently, until very lightly browned, about 5 minutes. Stir in the pineapple juice and vanilla bean. Decrease the heat to low and simmer until the liquid is reduced by half, 4 to 5 minutes. Remove from the heat. Carefully remove the vanilla bean, scrape the seeds back into the skillet, and discard the bean.

When the plantains are done, carefully peel them one at a time, holding each in a clean folded dish towel to protect your hand from the heat. Slice the plantains into ¼-inch-thick rounds and distribute among four serving bowls. Divide the pineapple mixture over the plantains and top each serving with ½ cup of the granola. Serve immediately.

Per serving: calories: 732.5, protein: 14.8 g, carbohydrates: 143.4 g, fat: 15.4 g, calcium: 76.4 mg, sodium: 22.2 mg, omega-3: 0.2 g

Scrambled Tofu and Curried Potatoes

YIELD: 6 SERVINGS

IN ADDITION TO SOME DELIGHTFULLY UNCONVENTIONAL BREAKFAST FLAVORS, *this recipe dishes up hearty complex carbohydrates and protein to start your day off right.*

2 yellow onions, diced

6 stalks celery, diced

2 tablespoons chopped garlic

I shallot, finely diced

I tablespoon mild curry powder

4 medium russet potatoes, peeled and diced

I ½ cups vegetable broth (preferably homemade, page 28)

2 packages (14 ounces each) firm tofu, drained and diced

I tablespoon chopped fresh thyme

2 green onions (white and green parts), thinly sliced on an angle, for garnish

Heat a medium saucepan over medium heat for 1 minute. Put the onions, half of the celery, and the garlic and shallot in the saucepan and cook, stirring frequently, until the vegetables soften and the onions become golden, about 5 minutes. Add the curry powder and cook, stirring constantly, for 1 minute. Add the potatoes and cook, stirring frequently, for 2 minutes. Stir in the broth, cover, and decrease the heat to low. Cook until the potatoes are fork-tender, 10 to 15 minutes. Add the remaining celery and the tofu and thyme and stir until well combined. Cook, stirring frequently, until the celery starts to soften and the tofu is heated through, about 10 minutes. Remove from the heat. Serve immediately, garnished with the green onions.

Per serving: calories: 335.9, protein: 23.1 g, carbohydrates: 45.6 g, fat: 7.5 g, calcium: 153.3 mg, sodium: 158.8 mg, omega-3: 0 g

Breakfast Potatoes

THIS IS A WHOLESOME ALTERNATIVE TO THE GREASY FRIED AND OVERLY SALTED POTATO DISHES *often served at breakfast time. This dish can be prepared ahead of time, so all you need to do is bake it before serving.*

8 medium russet potatoes, scrubbed

2 cups small cauliflower florets

2 cups quartered white mushrooms

6 Roma tomatoes, cubed

1 small yellow onion, diced

¼ teaspoon granulated garlic

¼ teaspoon granulated onion

3 tablespoons chopped fresh basil, or 1 tablespoon dried

3 tablespoons chopped fresh parsley, or 1 tablespoon dried

Preheat the oven to 350 degrees F.

Pierce each potato a few times with a fork or paring knife. Put the potatoes directly on a rack in the center of the oven and bake for 45 minutes, or until tender. The potatoes are done when a paring knife can be easily inserted in the center. Turn off the oven. Transfer the potatoes to a cooling rack.

When the potatoes are cool to the touch, peel and dice them. Line a rimmed baking sheet with parchment paper. Arrange the potatoes on the lined baking sheet. Scatter the cauliflower, mushrooms, tomatoes, and onion over the potatoes. Sprinkle with the granulated garlic and granulated onion. (At this point, the baking sheet can be covered with plastic wrap and refrigerated for 8 to 12 hours. When you are ready to bake the dish, bring the vegetables to room temperature while you preheat the oven. Remove the plastic wrap before baking.)

Preheat the oven to 350 degrees F.

Bake for 12 to 15 minutes, until all the vegetables start to brown. Remove from the oven and sprinkle with the basil and parsley. Serve hot.

NOTE: It takes about 1 hour for the baked potatoes to cool down enough to be peeled. For speed and convenience, the potatoes can be baked 1 day in advance and stored in the refrigerator.

Per serving: calories: 276.4, protein: 9.1 g, carbohydrates: 62.4 g, fat: 0.7 g, calcium: 76.7 mg, sodium: 37.8 mg, omega-3: 0.1 g

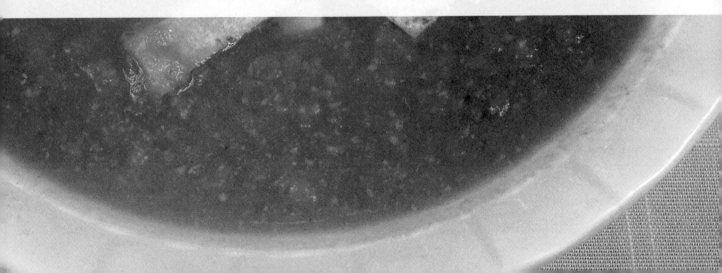

CHAPTER 4
Soups

SOUPS CAN BE AN IMPORTANT PART OF YOUR NEW HEALTHFUL DIET. They are easy to make, easy to store in the refrigerator or freezer, and easy to reheat. Soups feature prominently in my Daily Menus (see chapter 1, pages 14 to 20) because they combine well with other dishes to make hearty, satisfying, and nutritious meals.

Here are a few simple tips that will make your soups stand out. Always use vegetable broth, not water, as your liquid. Using water will result in a bland soup. In addition, high-quality ingredients will result in a more flavorful soup. Since soups develop more intense flavor after about twenty-four hours, make them a day ahead, if possible. Consider making a large quantity so you will have enough for a few meals; having soup on hand can be a real time-saver. Soups that are processed in a blender may separate after they are stored and reheated, but reprocessing reheated soups for a few seconds will restore the smooth consistency.

Cream of Asparagus Soup

YOU CAN MAKE THIS DELICATELY FLAVORED SOUP YEAR-ROUND, *but the best time to make it is during asparagus season, from March to June.*

6 cups vegetable broth (preferably homemade, page 28)

1 yellow onion, diced

1 leek (see page 27), thinly sliced

½ small fennel bulb, diced

2 cloves garlic, chopped

1 shallot, diced

1 pound asparagus

1 cup fresh spinach leaves, stemmed and firmly packed

1 cup water

1 cup unsweetened soymilk

Put ¼ cup of the broth and the onion, leek, fennel, garlic, and shallot in a medium pot over medium heat. Cook, stirring occasionally, for 10 minutes. Do not brown the vegetables.

Cut the upper tips off the asparagus stalks and set the tips aside. Cut 1 inch off the bottom of the asparagus stalks and discard the bottoms. Slice the stalks into 1-inch pieces, add them to the pot, and cook for 5 minutes. Add the remaining 5¾ cups of broth, increase the heat to medium-high, and simmer, stirring occasionally, for 20 minutes.

Meanwhile, put the spinach and water in a blender and process on high speed until completely smooth and even in color, with no flecks of green remaining. Strain through a coffee filter. Reserve the liquid and discard the filter and its contents. Pour the liquid into a small saucepan over medium-low heat and bring to a simmer. Use a ladle to skim off all the green foam that forms on the surface and put the foam in a small bowl. Discard the remaining liquid.

When the soup is finished cooking, stir in the soymilk and the spinach foam. Transfer to a blender and process on high speed until smooth. Strain through a fine-mesh strainer into a large bowl. Pour into a clean pot (or rinse out the pot used earlier). Bring to a simmer over medium-high heat. Stir in the asparagus tips and simmer for 1 minute. Serve hot.

Stored in a sealed container in the refrigerator, Cream of Asparagus Soup will keep for 3 days. Reheat before serving.

NOTE: The spinach foam can be omitted from the recipe to save time. However, the soup won't be as vibrantly green.

Per serving: calories: 123.2, protein: 7.1 g, carbohydrates: 23.6 g, fat: 1.5 g, calcium: 185.7 mg, sodium: 160.9 mg, omega-3: 0.1 g

Creamy Cauliflower Soup

THIS REFRESHINGLY LIGHT SOUP GOES WELL WITH MANY DISHES. *Cauliflower is available year-round, so you can turn to this recipe whenever you need a light-colored soup to accent a meal.*

I large cauliflower, cut into small florets

I onion, diced

I small celery root, peeled and diced

I small turnip, peeled and diced

I stalk celery, diced

I shallot, diced

I clove garlic, chopped

¼ teaspoon red pepper flakes (optional)

5 cups vegetable broth (preferably homemade, page 28)

I cup unsweetened soymilk

Ground nutmeg, for garnish

Preheat the oven to 350 degrees F. Line a rimmed baking sheet with parchment paper.

Put ½ cup of the cauliflower florets on the lined baking sheet and roast for 40 to 45 minutes, until lightly browned.

Put the remaining cauliflower and the onion, celery root, turnip, celery, shallot, garlic, red pepper flakes, and ¼ cup of the broth in a large pot over medium-low heat. Cook, stirring occasionally, for 10 minutes. Do not allow the bottom of the pot to brown. Stir in the remaining 4¾ cups of broth and the soymilk. Increase the heat to medium-high and bring to a simmer. Decrease the heat to medium and cook, stirring occasionally, for 15 minutes. Transfer to a blender and process on high speed until smooth. You may need to process the soup in batches depending on the size of your blender. Serve hot, garnished with the roasted cauliflower and nutmeg.

Stored in a sealed container in the refrigerator, Creamy Cauliflower Soup will keep for 3 days. Reheat and garnish just before serving.

NOTE: Choose firm, white cauliflower, without any brown spots or yellow leaves.

Per serving: calories: 193.1, protein: 9.7 g, carbohydrates: 39.2 g, fat: 1.8 g, calcium: 221 mg, sodium: 333.5 mg, omega-3: 0.1 g

Creamy Sunchoke Soup with Watercress

YIELD: 6 SERVINGS

SUNCHOKES HAVE A WONDERFULLY NUTTY TASTE THAT IS SURE TO DELIGHT. *This soup goes well with a wide variety of vegetables, grains, and other dishes.*

8 cups vegetable broth (preferably homemade, page 28)

2 leeks (see page 27), thinly sliced

1 yellow onion, diced

2 stalks celery, diced

2 shallots, diced

2 cloves garlic, chopped

6 cups peeled and coarsely chopped sunchokes

1½ cups unsweetened soymilk

2 cups Polenta Croutons (page 32), baked

6 ounces watercress, washed and stemmed

Put ¼ cup of the broth and the leeks, onion, celery, shallots, and garlic in a large pot and over medium heat. Cook, stirring occasionally, for about 5 minutes. Do not brown the vegetables. Stir in the sunchokes and the remaining 7¾ cups of broth. Increase the heat to medium-high and bring to a simmer. Stir in the soymilk and return to a simmer. Cook for 20 minutes, using a ladle to skim off any foam that forms at the surface. Discard the foam.

Transfer the soup to a blender and process on high speed until smooth. You may need to process the soup in batches depending on the size of your blender. Serve immediately, topped with the croutons and watercress.

NOTE: Sunchokes are also known as jerusalem artichokes. Because they turn brown quickly after they are peeled, it's best to cook them as soon as possible.

Per serving: calories: 261.3, protein: 8.4 g, carbohydrates: 56.4 g, fat: 1.7 g, calcium: 166.5 mg, sodium: 166 mg, omega-3: 0 g

Kabocha Squash and Yellow Curry Soup

YIELD: 6 SERVINGS

RECIPES THAT COMBINE WINTER SQUASH WITH CURRY SEASONINGS *are very popular in Asian countries. The combination works great because the sweet and spicy flavors are an ideal complement.*

2 kabocha squash, about 3 pounds each

I cup sliced celery

I cup sliced red onion

I cup sliced yellow onion

2 tablespoons peeled and chopped fresh ginger

2 tablespoons chopped shallot

I tablespoon chopped garlic

2 teaspoons curry powder

½ cup coconut milk

8 cups Asian Broth (page 30)

2 medium Yukon gold potatoes, peeled and diced

I medium yam, peeled and diced

I cup diced firm tofu

I teaspoon black sesame seeds, for garnish

Cilantro sprigs, for garnish

Preheat the oven to 400 degrees F. Line a rimmed baking sheet with parchment paper.

Cut the squash in half and scoop out the seeds with a metal spoon. Put the squash cut-side down on the lined baking sheet and bake for about 30 minutes, until soft when pierced with a fork. When cool enough to handle, scoop out the pulp and set aside.

Put the celery, red and yellow onions, ginger, shallot, and garlic in a large dry pot over medium heat and cook, stirring occasionally, for 5 minutes. Stir in the curry powder and cook for 2 minutes. Stir in the coconut milk and cook for 2 minutes. Stir in the squash pulp, broth, potatoes, and yam. Increase the heat to medium-high and bring to a simmer. Decrease the heat to medium and cook uncovered, stirring occasionally, until the potatoes and yam are fork-tender, 10 to 15 minutes. Stir in the tofu and simmer for 2 minutes. Serve hot, garnished with the sesame seeds and cilantro sprigs.

Stored in a sealed container in the refrigerator, Kabocha Squash and Yellow Curry Soup will keep for 3 days. Reheat and garnish just before serving.

Per serving: calories: 354, protein: 10.2 g, carbohydrates: 69.6 g, fat: 7 g, calcium: 172.9 mg, sodium: 132 mg, omega-3: 0.1 g

Potato-Leek Soup

YIELD: 4 SERVINGS

THIS WONDERFULLY FRAGRANT SOUP *is sure to please family and friends. Its delicate taste and texture make it perfect for light meals or as an accent to other dishes.*

2 large Yukon gold potatoes, scrubbed and diced

4 leeks (see page 27), thinly sliced

2 shallots, chopped

I stalk celery, thinly sliced

I clove garlic, chopped

6 cups vegetable broth (preferably homemade, page 28)

2 bay leaves

I tablespoon chopped fresh thyme, or I teaspoon dried

2 tablespoons chopped fresh chives, for garnish

Preheat the oven to 350 degrees F. Line a rimmed baking sheet with parchment paper.

Put the potatoes on the lined baking sheet and bake for about 20 minutes, or until well browned.

Put the leeks, shallots, celery, and garlic in a medium dry pot over medium heat and cook for 5 minutes, stirring occasionally. Stir in the potatoes, broth, and bay leaves. Increase the heat to medium-high and bring to a simmer. Decrease the heat to medium-low, cover, and cook, stirring occasionally, for 20 minutes. Add the thyme, cover, and cook, stirring occasionally, for 5 minutes. Remove the bay leaves and serve hot, garnished with the chives.

Stored in a sealed container in the refrigerator, Potato-Leek Soup will keep for 3 days. Reheat and garnish just before serving.

NOTE: For a smoother texture, process the soup in a blender before serving.

Per serving: calories: 237.4, protein: 6.7 g, carbohydrates: 54.6 g, fat: 0.4 g, calcium: 88.7 mg, sodium: 116.5 mg, omega-3: 0.1 g

Mucha Onion Soup

THIS IS A GREAT ALTERNATIVE TO FRENCH ONION SOUP. *Be sure to pay close attention throughout the entire cooking process to avoid burning the onions and achieve the right flavor.*

2 cups sliced leeks (see page 27)

2 cups sliced red onions

2 cups diced yellow onions

1 cup sliced celery

1 cup chopped shallots

¼ cup chopped garlic

12 cups vegetable broth (preferably homemade, page 28)

3 tablespoons brown rice vinegar

2 tablespoons chopped fresh chives, for garnish

Heat a large pot on medium heat for 2 minutes. Put the leeks, red and yellow onions, celery, shallots, and garlic in the pot. Cook, stirring occasionally, until the vegetables start to brown and stick to the bottom of the pot, about 5 minutes. Stir in 2 tablespoons of the broth and use the spoon to loosen any bits that are stuck to the bottom of the pot. Continue browning the vegetables for 5 minutes, stirring frequently. Stir in 2 more tablespoons of broth and once again loosen any bits that are stuck to the pot. Continue to brown the vegetables and add broth in this fashion, decreasing the heat a bit each time; the more often you repeat these steps, the richer the flavor of the soup will be. Continue until the onions turn a deep brown but are not burnt. Stir in the vinegar and use the spoon to loosen any bits that are stuck to the pot. Stir in the remaining broth and increase the heat to high. Bring to a boil, decrease the heat to medium–low, and simmer uncovered for 20 minutes, stirring occasionally. Serve hot, garnished with the chives.

Stored in a sealed container in the refrigerator, Mucha Onion Soup will keep for 3 days. Reheat and garnish just before serving.

NOTE: Taste the soup before serving. If it's not tart enough, stir in more vinegar as desired.

Per serving: calories: 138.6, protein: 4.1 g, carbohydrates: 31.5 g, fat: 0.4 g, calcium: 104 mg, sodium: 191.9 mg, omega-3: 0.1 g

Tortilla Soup

SEE PHOTO ON FACING PAGE   YIELD: 6 SERVINGS

ONE OF MY EARLIEST FOOD MEMORIES IS HAVING TORTILLA SOUP *from my grandmother's kitchen. Corn tortillas are easily available in most supermarkets. White corn tortillas are more common than yellow ones, but either kind will work.*

6 corn tortillas

Kernels sliced from 2 ears fresh corn (see page 27), or 2 cups thawed frozen or drained canned corn

3 stalks celery, diced

1 carrot, scrubbed and diced

3 shallots, chopped

3 cloves garlic, thinly sliced

1½ teaspoons dried oregano

½ teaspoon granulated garlic

½ teaspoon granulated onion

5 Roma tomatoes

2 medium potatoes, peeled and diced

12 cups vegetable broth (preferably homemade, page 28)

10 fresh epazote leaves, sliced into strips (optional)

2 ripe avocados, sliced, for garnish

10 sprigs cilantro, for garnish

1 lime, sliced into 6 wedges, for garnish

Preheat the oven to 350 degrees F.

Slice the tortillas into small strips. Arrange them in a single layer on a baking sheet and bake for about 10 minutes, until crispy.

Put the corn, celery, carrot, shallots, and garlic in a large dry pot and cook over medium heat for 5 minutes, stirring occasionally. Stir in the oregano, granulated garlic, and granulated onion and cook, stirring frequently, for 5 minutes. Put the tomatoes in a blender and process on high speed until smooth. Add the tomatoes and potatoes to the pot and cook, stirring occasionally, for 5 minutes. Stir in the broth and increase the heat to medium-high. Simmer for 15 minutes. Stir in the optional epazote and simmer for 5 minutes.

Ladle into soup bowls and garnish with the avocado, cilantro sprigs, and lime. Top with the tortilla strips. Serve immediately.

NOTE: This recipe results in a brothlike soup. For a thick and creamy soup, put the soup and the baked tortilla strips in a blender and process on high speed until smooth. Serve immediately, garnished with the avocado, cilantro sprigs, and lime.

Per serving: calories: 269, protein: 6.7 g, carbohydrates: 47.2 g, fat: 8.3 g, calcium: 99.5 mg, sodium: 147.9 mg, omega-3: 0.1 g

Tortilla Soup

Yellow Corn Chowder

Yellow Corn Chowder

SEE PHOTO ON FACING PAGE YIELD: 6 SERVINGS

IF YOU ARE YEARNING FOR A SWEET SOUP WITH A CHEWY TEXTURE, *this recipe will fit the bill. You can make it year-round, but fresh corn is sweetest in late summer and early fall.*

2 leeks (see page 27), thinly sliced

3 shallots, thinly sliced

4 cloves garlic, minced

Kernels sliced from 4 ears fresh corn (see page 27), or 4 cups thawed frozen or drained canned corn

2 medium yellow potatoes, peeled and diced

2 stalks celery, thinly sliced

¼ teaspoon red pepper flakes (optional)

6 cups vegetable broth (preferably homemade, page 28)

I cup unsweetened soymilk

I tablespoon chopped fresh chives, or I teaspoon dried

I tablespoon chopped fresh thyme, or I teaspoon dried

Put the leeks, shallots, and garlic in a medium dry pot over medium-low heat and cook, stirring occasionally, for 5 minutes. Stir in the corn, potatoes, celery, and red pepper flakes. Cook, stirring frequently, for 15 minutes, making sure the vegetables don't brown. Stir in the broth and soymilk. Increase the heat to medium-high and simmer for 20 minutes, using a ladle to skim off any foam that forms at the surface. Discard the foam. Stir in the chives and thyme. Serve hot.

Stored in a sealed container in the refrigerator, Yellow Corn Chowder will keep for 3 days. Reheat before serving.

NOTE: If you replace the yellow corn with sweet white corn, this soup will taste just as good. I prefer yellow corn for this recipe because the color contrasts so well with the other ingredients.

Per serving: calories: 178.1, protein: 6.2 g, carbohydrates: 38 g, fat: 1.6 g, calcium: 101.1 mg, sodium: 106.5 mg, omega-3: 0 g

Wild Mushroom Soup

YIELD: 4 SERVINGS

THIS RECIPE USES SOME OF THE MORE WIDELY AVAILABLE MUSHROOMS. *Many other varieties, including chanterelle (my personal favorite), hedgehog, maitake (also called hen of the woods), morel, porcini, or trumpet, can be used as well.*

2 cups sliced cremini mushrooms

2 cups sliced oyster mushrooms

2 cups sliced portobello mushrooms

2 cups sliced shiitake mushrooms

I small red onion, diced

I small yellow onion, diced

I tablespoon chopped fresh epazote, or I teaspoon dried (optional)

I tablespoon chopped fresh parsley

I tablespoon chopped fresh thyme, or I teaspoon dried

6½ cups vegetable broth (preferably homemade, page 28)

Preheat the oven to 350 degrees F. Line a rimmed baking sheet with parchment paper.

Put the cremini, oyster, portobello, and shiitake mushrooms, half of the red and yellow onions, the optional epazote, parsley, thyme, and ½ cup of the broth in a large bowl and stir to combine. Transfer to the lined baking sheet, arrange in a single layer, and bake for 12 minutes, until the mushrooms start to release their juices.

Put the remaining red and yellow onions and the leek, shallot, and garlic in a large dry pot over medium heat and cook, stirring occasionally, until the mixture is lightly browned, about 5 minutes. Stir in the vinegar and use the spoon to loosen any bits that are stuck to the bottom of the pot. Cook, stirring frequently, until the mixture is more deeply browned, 5 to 10 minutes longer. Add the mushroom mixture and any juices left on the baking sheet (it's all mushroom flavor, so don't waste it) and cook, stirring occasionally, for 5 minutes. Stir in the remaining 6 cups of the broth. Increase the heat to medium-high and bring to a simmer. Decrease the heat to medium and cook, stirring occasionally, for 20 minutes. Serve hot, garnished with the chives and enoki mushrooms.

1 small leek (see page 27), thinly sliced

1 tablespoon chopped shallot

1½ teaspoons chopped garlic

2 tablespoons brown rice vinegar

2 tablespoons chopped fresh chives, for garnish

2 ounces enoki mushrooms, trimmed, for garnish

Stored in a sealed container in the refrigerator, Wild Mushroom Soup will keep for 3 days. Reheat and garnish just before serving.

NOTE: If you prefer, this soup can be made with only one kind of mushroom. Using a variety, however, adds a bit more interest and substance.

Per serving: calories: 114.8, protein: 5.6 g, carbohydrates: 24.6 g, fat: 0.6 g, calcium: 34.2 mg, sodium: 102.4 mg, omega-3: 0 g

Sea Vegetable and Baked Rice Soup

YIELD: 6 SERVINGS

THIS RECIPE WAS INSPIRED BY THE SIZZLING RICE SOUP *that is served in many Chinese restaurants. The sizzling effect can't be achieved in this recipe because the rice isn't fried, but the soup is flavorful and much more nutritious.*

1 cup cooked brown rice (see page 25), completely cooled

2 cups sliced shiitake mushrooms

½ cup diced celery

½ cup sliced shallots

2 tablespoons peeled and thinly sliced ginger

Kernels sliced from 2 ears fresh corn (see page 27), or 2 cups thawed frozen or drained canned corn

1 strip kombu

8 cups Asian Broth (page 30)

2 cups diced firm tofu

1 cup sugar snap peas, trimmed

1 small carrot, scrubbed and grated

1 tablespoon sesame seeds, toasted (see page 26)

6 sheets nori, cut into 2-inch strips, for garnish

12 sprigs cilantro, for garnish

Preheat the oven to 350 degrees F. Line a rimmed baking sheet with parchment paper.

Spread the rice in a single layer on the lined baking sheet and bake, stirring occasionally, for about 20 minutes, until crispy and golden brown. Break up any rice clumps to ensure that all the rice becomes crispy.

Put the mushrooms, celery, shallots, and ginger in a large dry pot over medium heat and cook for 5 minutes, stirring occasionally. Stir in the corn, kombu, and broth. Increase the heat to medium-high and simmer, stirring occasionally, for 15 minutes. Remove the kombu, cut it into 1-inch strips, and return the strips to the soup. Stir in the tofu, sugar snap peas, carrot, and sesame seeds and simmer for 2 minutes. Ladle into soup bowls and garnish each serving with the baked rice, nori strips, and cilantro sprigs. Serve immediately.

NOTE: Kombu will expand to about four times its size when simmered.

Per serving: calories: 166.5, protein: 8.9 g, carbohydrates: 27.3 g, fat: 3.5 g, calcium: 49.6 mg, sodium: 116.1 mg, omega-3: 0 g

CHAPTER 5

Salads

S OME PEOPLE MAY THINK OF SALAD AS WILTED LETTUCE with paper-thin slices of tomato and onion that is served before the "real" food. That's not what I call salad. Rather, I envision crisp lettuces and a variety of colorful, succulent vegetables tossed with one of my gourmet dressings (pages 68 to 74). But you can dream up those combinations on your own.

In this chapter, I present unconventional salad recipes (none even contains lettuce) that feature a variety of flavors and textures. My favorite is the Hawaiian Salad (page 64), which is made with tender cabbage, earthy cilantro, tart grapefruits, spicy ginger, crunchy jicama, savory macadamia nuts, sweet mangoes, and even a pinch of sesame seeds. I give you the task of finding your own favorite recipe in this chapter. As you explore, I suspect your taste buds will be dancing with every bite.

Fresh Herb and Strawberry Salad

YIELD: 4 SERVINGS

FRESH HERBS MAKE THIS GOURMET SALAD EXQUISITE. *But don't save it just for special occasions. Serve it frequently. What is stopping you from making your life one long, continuous special occasion?*

4 cups fresh strawberries, hulled and cut in half lengthwise

1 bulb fennel, grated or thinly shaved with a mandoline

2 stalks celery, grated or thinly shaved with a mandoline

1 cup fresh basil leaves, lightly packed

1 cup fresh mint leaves, lightly packed

1 cup fresh flat-leaf parsley leaves, lightly packed

½ cup sliced fresh chives, in 1-inch pieces

½ cup Raspberry-Walnut Dressing (page 70)

½ cup whole walnuts, toasted (see page 26)

Put the strawberries, fennel, celery, basil, mint, parsley, and chives in a large bowl. Add the dressing and toss until evenly distributed. Spoon into salad bowls and sprinkle with the walnuts. Serve immediately.

NOTE: It is important that the herbs in this salad be as fresh as possible and that the salad be eaten shortly after it is made. Farmers' markets are the ideal place to purchase fresh herbs.

Per serving: calories: 197.8, protein: 6.3 g, carbohydrates: 25.1 g, fat: 10.5 g, calcium: 183.9 mg, sodium: 69.1 mg, omega-3: 1.5 g

VARIATION: Replace the strawberries with blackberries or other berries. The salad will be just as delicious.

Beet and Citrus Salad

THIS COLORFUL SALAD IS DELICIOUSLY SWEET. *Beets are a great source of potassium and can often be purchased with their leaves attached. The leaves can be refrigerated and saved for another meal; simply steam or sauté them for a nutritious side dish.*

2 large chioggia beets, scrubbed

2 large golden beets, scrubbed

4 large oranges, peeled and cut into half-moons

2 grapefruits, segmented

1 medium jicama, peeled and diced

4 ounces baby arugula

1 stalk celery with leaves, diced

¼ cup pumpkin seeds, toasted (see page 26)

Steam the chioggia and golden beets (see Steaming Vegetables, page 24) until a paring knife inserted in the center of a beet can be removed without resistance. Let cool. When cool enough to handle, peel the beets by rubbing off the skin with your fingers and slice the beets into half-moons.

Put the beets, oranges, grapefruits, jicama, arugula, and celery in a large bowl and toss until well combined. Spoon into salad bowls and sprinkle with the pumpkin seeds. Serve immediately.

NOTE: Red beets can be used to replace the chioggia and golden beets. However, the red color will bleed, and the salad will not have the same attractive appearance.

Per serving: calories: 292.3, protein: 7.7 g, carbohydrates: 59.5 g, fat: 4.7 g, calcium: 138.5 mg, sodium: 130.8 mg, omega-3: 0.1 g

Chayote-Apple Slaw

YIELD: 6 SERVINGS

THIS LIGHT, SWEET SALAD IS A TRUE DELIGHT. *The cashews provide crunch and healthful calories.*

2 Granny Smith apples with peel, sliced

2 Fuji or Gala apples with peel, sliced

Juice of 2 lemons

4 chayotes, peeled and cut into strips

I small jicama, peeled and cubed

I stalk celery with leaves, sliced

I tablespoon chopped fresh thyme, or I teaspoon dried

½ teaspoon celery seeds

½ cup cashews halves, toasted (see page 26)

Put the Granny Smith and Fuji apples in a large bowl. Stir in the lemon juice to prevent browning. Add the chayotes, jicama, celery, thyme, and celery seeds and toss until well combined. Spoon into salad bowls and sprinkle with the cashews. Serve immediately.

NOTE: There are two varieties of chayote: one with prickly skin and one with smooth skin. Both types can be found at most Latin markets, and either can be used in this recipe. Their taste has been likened to a combination of cucumber and jicama. Be sure to wear kitchen gloves when you peel them, because exposure to the skins can dry out your hands.

Per serving: calories: 182.8, protein: 4.2 g, carbohydrates: 33.7 g, fat: 5.5 g, calcium: 51.5 mg, sodium: 25 mg, omega-3: 0.1 g

Bravo Coleslaw

YIELD: 4 SERVINGS

THIS IS A TASTY AND HEALTHFUL ALTERNATIVE TO CONVENTIONAL COLESLAWS, *which are typically loaded with mayonnaise and salt.*

4 cups finely shredded napa cabbage

2 Gala apples, diced

I cup finely shredded red cabbage

2 small carrots, peeled and sliced into thin strips

Juice of 4 lemons

½ cup pine nuts, toasted (see page 26)

Put the napa cabbage, apples, red cabbage, carrots, and lemon juice in a large bowl and toss until well combined. Let marinate in the refrigerator for at least 1 hour before serving or for up to 3 days. Just before serving, spoon into salad bowls and sprinkle with the pine nuts.

Per serving: calories: 201.2, protein: 5.1 g, carbohydrates: 23.8 g, fat: 12 g, calcium: 79.8 mg, sodium: 47 mg, omega-3: 0 g

Broccoli Slaw

YIELD: 4 SERVINGS

THIS SLAW IS SWEET AND CRUNCHY *and provides a great way to use the broccoli stems that many people throw away.*

4 broccoli stems, peeled and thinly sliced with a mandoline

2 nectarines with skin, diced

1 celery heart, or 3 to 4 stalks celery with leaves, chopped

1 cup thinly sliced red cabbage

Juice of 2 oranges

30 fresh mint leaves

½ cup almonds with skins, toasted (see page 26) and coarsely chopped

Put the broccoli, nectarines, celery, cabbage, orange juice, and mint (see note) in a large bowl and toss until well combined. To serve immediately, spoon into salad bowls and sprinkle with the almonds. Stored in a sealed container in the refrigerator, Broccoli Slaw, without the mint and almonds, will keep for 2 days. Add the mint and sprinkle with the almonds just before serving.

NOTE: Because the acid in the orange juice will quickly turn the mint brown, stir in the mint just before serving.

Per serving: calories: 162.7, protein: 7.5 g, carbohydrates: 23.1 g, fat: 6.7 g, calcium: 117.8 mg, sodium: 62.9 mg, omega-3: 0.2 g

Celery Root Slaw

YIELD: 6 SERVINGS

CELERY ROOT, ALSO KNOWN AS CELERIAC, IS A HIGHLY VERSATILE VEGETABLE. *Although it is used raw in this recipe, it can be cooked in just about every way possible. Celery root tastes like a combination of celery and parsley.*

4 celery roots (each about 1 pound), peeled, rinsed, and cut into thin strips

1½ cups freshly squeezed orange juice

4 fuyu persimmons, sliced into half-moons (peeling is optional)

1 large pomegranate, quartered and seeds removed

30 fresh mint leaves

1 cup pecans, toasted (see page 26)

Put the celery roots in a large bowl. Stir in the orange juice to prevent browning. Add the persimmons, pomegranate seeds, and mint and toss until well combined. To serve immediately, spoon into salad bowls and sprinkle with the pecans. Stored in a sealed container in the refrigerator, Celery Root Slaw, without the pecans, will keep for 2 days. Sprinkle with the pecans just before serving.

NOTE: I suggest wearing an old apron when working with pomegranates, because the juice can get all over your clothes. Be sure to avoid using any of the bitter white membrane.

Per serving: calories: 332.7, protein: 5.9 g, carbohydrates: 54.5 g, fat: 13.3 g, calcium: 100.1 mg, sodium: 159.5 mg, omega-3: 0.2 g

SUMMER CELERY ROOT SLAW: Replace the persimmons with peaches, the pomegranate with grapes, and the pecans with pistachios.

Pickled Vegetable Slaw

THIS REFRESHING SALAD HAS AN INTRIGUING "BITE" *that makes it a delightful complement to all kinds of vegetable dishes.*

1½ cups brown rice vinegar

2 shallots, very thinly sliced

1 head green cabbage (about 2 pounds), very thinly sliced

3 small bulbs fennel, very thinly sliced

6 stalks celery, very thinly sliced

1 large carrot, scrubbed and very thinly sliced

1½ teaspoons celery seeds

20 sprigs flat-leaf parsley, stemmed and chopped

20 fresh basil leaves, thinly sliced

¼ cup chopped fresh chives

Freshly ground pepper

Put the vinegar and shallots in a small bowl and stir to combine. Put the cabbage, fennel, celery, and carrot in a large bowl and toss until combined. Stir in the shallots, vinegar, and celery seeds. Let marinate in the refrigerator for at least 10 minutes or up to 2 hours. Add the parsley, basil, and chives and toss until well combined. Season with pepper to taste. Serve immediately.

NOTE: Because the acid in the vinegar will quickly turn the herbs brown, stir in the parsley, basil, and chives just before serving.

Per serving: calories: 117.3, protein: 4.5 g, carbohydrates: 24.6 g, fat: 0.5 g, calcium: 145.8 mg, sodium: 123.9 mg, omega–3: 0 g

Hawaiian Salad

SEE PHOTO ON FRONT COVER   YIELD: 4 SERVINGS

WHERE I LIVED ON THE ISLAND OF OAHU, *all the ingredients in this recipe were used in local restaurants. Although they are not all native to Hawaii (not even macadamias), the ingredients complement each other perfectly.*

2 small jicamas, peeled and cut into matchsticks

2 ruby grapefruits, segmented

½ head green cabbage, finely shredded

I mango, diced

½ cup whole macadamia nuts, toasted (see page 26)

10 sprigs cilantro, stemmed

I tablespoon sesame seeds, toasted (see page 26)

I cup Mango-Ginger Dressing (page 68)

Put the jicamas, grapefruits, cabbage, mango, nuts, cilantro, and sesame seeds in a large bowl. Cover and refrigerate for up to 2 days. Just before serving, add the dressing and toss until evenly distributed.

Per serving: calories: 370.8, protein: 6.2 g, carbohydrates: 60.3 g, fat: 15 g, calcium: 153.4 mg, sodium: 33.2 mg, omega-3: 0.1 g

Mixed Sprouts and Kelp Noodle Salad

YIELD: 4 SERVINGS

THE SPROUTS GIVE THIS SALAD A CRUNCHY TEXTURE *and the kelp noodles lend a slightly salty flavor.*

3 quarts mixed sprouts (such as alfalfa, clover, lentil, mung, or sunflower sprouts or pea shoots), lightly packed

4 oranges, peeled and sliced

3 cups kelp noodles (see note), drained and put on paper towels to dry

½ cup Citrus-Tahini Dressing (page 70)

½ cup hazelnuts, toasted (see page 26)

Put the sprouts, oranges, kelp noodles, and dressing in a large bowl. Toss gently (avoid crushing the sprouts) until well combined. Spoon into salad bowls and sprinkle with the hazelnuts. Serve immediately.

NOTE: Kelp noodles are available at natural food stores and some high-end grocery stores.

Per serving: calories: 287.5, protein: 10.3 g, carbohydrates: 30 g, fat: 16.6 g, calcium: 169.1 mg, sodium: 55 mg, omega-3: 0.2 g

Hearts of Palm Salad

THIS SWEET-AND-SOUR SALAD *pairs nicely with a wide variety of dishes.*

½ cup brown rice vinegar

I shallot, minced

I can (14 ounces) hearts of palm (see note), drained, rinsed, and cut into strips

2 cucumbers, peeled and cut into strips

I small jicama, peeled and diced

I small ripe papaya (see notes), diced

I large ripe avocado, diced

¼ cup pumpkin seeds, toasted (see page 26)

Put the vinegar and shallot in a large bowl and stir to combine. Add the hearts of palm, cucumbers, jicama, papaya, and avocado and toss gently until well combined. Spoon into salad bowls and sprinkle with the pumpkin seeds. Serve immediately.

NOTES

- Canned hearts of palm can be purchased in either organic or conventional form at most supermarkets. They usually contain a large amount of sodium, which can be extracted by soaking the hearts of palm in distilled water for 20 minutes. Drain before using.

- Ripe papayas have bright yellowish-orange skin and a sweet aroma. They should be soft but not squishy.

Per serving: calories: 330, protein: 8.2 g, carbohydrates: 52.8 g, fat: 10.8 g, calcium: 75 mg, sodium: 31.2 mg, omega-3: 0.1 g

CHAPTER 6
Dressings

THE FLAVORFUL DRESSINGS IN THIS CHAPTER ARE MADE WITH WHOLESOME NATURAL FOODS and accented with subtle herbs and spices. You won't find added oil or salt in any of these dressings, and you won't miss them. To prove it, I suggest you try the following experiment.

Put a chopped apple, a chopped shallot, and about one-half cup of unsweetened apple juice in a blender and process on high speed until smooth. Now taste. You should detect apple and shallot. Now add two ounces of oil and process on high speed for about thirty seconds and taste again. The mixture will taste similar to the first mixture, only blander, and not as sharp. Now add a pinch or two of salt and process on high speed for another thirty seconds and taste. Once again, you'll detect the apple and shallot. The moral of the story is "Don't use oil and you won't need salt."

The dressings in this book have the most flavor and best consistency right after they are made. However, most of them will keep in the refrigerator for a few days. Each recipe indicates how long the dressing will keep.

Mango-Ginger Dressing

YIELD: 2 CUPS (8 SERVINGS)

A MANGO IS RIPE WHEN YOU CAN SMELL ITS SWEET FRAGRANCE.

2 ripe mangoes, coarsely chopped

I cup unsweetened apple juice

2 tablespoons peeled and chopped fresh ginger

I teaspoon brown rice vinegar

I tablespoon sesame seeds, toasted (see page 26)

Put the mangoes, apple juice, ginger, and vinegar in a blender and process on high speed until smooth. Stir in the sesame seeds until evenly distributed. Stored in a sealed container in the refrigerator, Mango-Ginger Dressing will keep for 4 days.

Per serving (¼ cup): calories: 55.7, protein: 0.5 g, carbohydrates: 12.8 g, fat: 0.8 g, calcium: 18.9 mg, sodium: 2.6 mg, omega-3: 0 g

Pineapple-Tarragon Dressing

YIELD: 2 CUPS (8 SERVINGS)

FRESH TARRAGON SHOULD ALWAYS BE BLANCHED *(see Blanching Herbs, page 26) to enhance its flavor and color.*

¼ fresh pineapple, cored and coarsely chopped, or I cup unsweetened canned pineapple chunks, juice reserved

¼ ripe papaya, seeded and coarsely chopped

I cup unsweetened pineapple juice (if using canned pineapple, include the reserved juice)

I½ teaspoons blanched fresh tarragon (see page 26), chopped, or ½ teaspoon dried

I½ teaspoons brown rice vinegar

½ teaspoon coriander seeds, toasted (see page 26)

Put all the ingredients in a blender and process on high speed until smooth. Stored in a sealed container in the refrigerator, Pineapple-Tarragon Dressing will keep for 3 days.

Per serving (¼ cup): calories: 34.4, protein: 0.3 g, carbohydrates: 8.7 g, fat: 0.1 g, calcium: 10 mg, sodium: 1.2 mg, omega-3: 0 g

Apple-Mustard Dressing

YIELD: 2 CUPS (8 SERVINGS)

SALT-FREE MUSTARD IS AVAILABLE AT NATURAL FOOD STORES AND GOURMET GROCERY STORES.

1½ cups peeled and coarsely chopped apples

¾ cup unsweetened apple juice

1½ tablespoons salt-free whole-grain mustard

1½ teaspoons cider vinegar

½ small shallot, peeled

4 fresh sage leaves, or ⅛ teaspoon dried

Put all the ingredients in a blender and process on high speed until smooth. Stored in a sealed container in the refrigerator, Apple-Mustard Dressing will keep for 4 days.

Per serving (¼ cup): calories: 12.9, protein: 0.1 g, carbohydrates: 3.3 g, fat: 0 g, calcium: 2.6 mg, sodium: 0.8 mg, omega-3: 0 g

Blood Orange Dressing

YIELD: 2 CUPS (8 SERVINGS)

BLOOD ORANGES, WHICH ARE USUALLY AVAILABLE DURING THE WINTER MONTHS, *have a tangy, vibrantly colored juice that makes this sweet-and-spicy dressing unforgettable.*

1 ripe pear, peeled and coarsely chopped

1½ cups freshly squeezed blood orange juice

½ shallot, coarsely chopped

½ teaspoon dried oregano

Put all the ingredients in a blender and process on high speed until smooth. Stored in a sealed container in the refrigerator, Blood Orange Dressing will keep for 3 days.

Per serving (¼ cup): calories: 39, protein: 0.6 g, carbohydrates: 9.5 g, fat: 0.1 g, calcium: 9.8 mg, sodium: 1.5 mg, omega-3: 0 g

Raspberry-Walnut Dressing

YIELD: 2 CUPS (8 SERVINGS)

FRESH RASPBERRIES ARE HIGHLY PERISHABLE. *They are usually sold in plastic containers. Before purchasing, inspect the paper that lines the container bottom. It should be dry, and the raspberries should not be bruised or moldy.*

6 ounces fresh or frozen raspberries

1 cup unsweetened apple juice

1 teaspoon brown rice vinegar

2 tablespoons walnuts

1 teaspoon dried oregano

Put the raspberries, apple juice, and vinegar in a blender and process on high speed until the raspberries are pulverized. Pour the mixture through a fine-mesh strainer to remove the raspberry seeds. Rinse the blender container to remove any seeds, then return the raspberry mixture to the container. Add the walnuts and oregano and process on high speed until smooth. Stored in a sealed container in the refrigerator, Raspberry-Walnut Dressing will keep for 2 days.

Per serving (¼ cup): calories: 48.8, protein: 0.8 g, carbohydrates: 6.6 g, fat: 2.5 g, calcium: 11.3 mg, sodium: 1.5 mg, omega-3: 0.4 g

Citrus-Tahini Dressing

YIELD: 2 CUPS (8 SERVINGS)

RAW TAHINI, WHICH IS MADE FROM SESAME SEEDS, *can be purchased at most natural food stores and gourmet grocery stores. This dressing is high in natural fat, so if you are accustomed to dressings that have a high oil content, this is a healthful choice that will feel satisfying and familiar.*

Juice of 2 oranges, seeds removed

Juice of 2 lemons, seeds removed

Juice of 2 limes, seeds removed

1 small shallot, peeled and coarsely chopped

6 tablespoons raw tahini

Put all the ingredients in a blender and process on high speed until smooth. Stored in a sealed container in the refrigerator, Citrus-Tahini Dressing will keep for 4 days.

Per serving (¼ cup): calories: 92, protein: 2.6 g, carbohydrates: 10.3 g, fat: 5.5 g, calcium: 66.3 mg, sodium: 9.8 mg, omega-3: 0 g

Avocado-Corn Dressing

YIELD: 2 CUPS (8 SERVINGS)

THE BEST WAY TO JUDGE THE RIPENESS OF AN AVOCADO IS TO REMOVE THE TINY STEM. *It should come off with no resistance, revealing a small green oval with no brown spots or veins showing.*

1 ripe avocado, flesh removed

Kernels sliced from 1 ear fresh corn (see page 27), or 1 cup thawed frozen or drained canned corn

1 cup vegetable broth (preferably homemade, page 28), plus more as needed

Juice of ¼ lime

10 sprigs cilantro, with stems

¼ teaspoon ground coriander

¼ teaspoon ground cumin

Put all the ingredients in a blender and process on high speed until smooth and creamy. If the dressing is too thick, add a little more broth, 1 to 2 tablespoons at a time, until the desired consistency is achieved. Stored in a sealed container in the refrigerator, Avocado-Corn Dressing will keep for 3 days.

Per serving (¼ cup): calories: 38.7, protein: 0.7 g, carbohydrates: 3.7 g, fat: 2.8 g, calcium: 2.6 mg, sodium: 9.4 mg, omega-3: 0 g

Tomato-Herb Dressing

YIELD: 2 CUPS (8 SERVINGS)

FRESH TOMATOES ARE AT THEIR BEST DURING SUMMER AND FALL. *That's the ideal time to make this dressing.*

2 large tomatoes, quartered

1 ½ teaspoons salt-free tomato paste

½ cup peeled and coarsely chopped cucumber

½ cup coarsely chopped fennel

1 tablespoon chopped fresh basil, or 1 teaspoon dried

1 tablespoon chopped fresh parsley, or 1 teaspoon dried

2 ¼ teaspoons dried oregano

1 ½ teaspoons chopped fresh chives, or ½ teaspoon dried

1 ½ teaspoons chopped fresh rosemary, or ½ teaspoon dried

1 ½ teaspoons chopped fresh thyme, or ½ teaspoon dried

Put the tomatoes and tomato paste in a blender and process on high speed until the tomatoes are pulverized. Pour the mixture through a fine-mesh strainer to remove the seeds and skins. Return the strained tomato mixture to the blender and add the cucumber, fennel, basil, parsley, oregano, chives, rosemary, and thyme. Process on low speed until smooth. Stored in a sealed container in the refrigerator, Tomato-Herb Dressing will keep for 3 days.

Per serving (¼ cup): calories: 15.7, protein: 0.7 g, carbohydrates: 3.4 g, fat: 0.2 g, calcium: 14.6 mg, sodium: 11.3 mg, omega-3: 0 g

Roasted Bell Pepper Dressing

YIELD: 2 CUPS (8 SERVINGS)

BECAUSE BELL PEPPERS ARE AVAILABLE YEAR-ROUND, *this dressing can be a staple. Although this recipe calls for red or yellow peppers, any color will work.*

2 large bell peppers (red, yellow, or both), halved, stemmed, and seeds and veins removed

½ cup vegetable broth (preferably homemade, page 28)

5 sprigs cilantro, with stems

½ shallot, peeled

½ teaspoon ground coriander

½ teaspoon ground cumin

Preheat the oven to 350 degrees F. Line a rimmed baking sheet with parchment paper.

Put the peppers cut-side down on the lined baking sheet and roast about 20 minutes, until the skins are browned. Let cool. When cool enough to handle, remove and discard the skins.

Put the peppers, broth, cilantro, shallot, coriander, and cumin in a blender and process on high speed until smooth. Stored in a sealed container in the refrigerator, Roasted Bell Pepper Dressing will keep for 3 days.

Per serving (¼ cup): calories: 17.8, protein: 0.6 g, carbohydrates: 3.7 g, fat: 0.1 g, calcium: 5.5 mg, sodium: 5.6 mg, omega-3: 0 g

Flaxseed Dressing

YIELD: 2 CUPS (8 SERVINGS)

FLAXSEEDS ARE A GREAT SOURCE OF OMEGA-3 FATTY ACIDS, *calcium, and iron. Store them in the refrigerator.*

¼ **acorn squash, seeds removed**

¾ **cup unsweetened apple juice**

½ **cup coarsely chopped celery**

2 **tablespoons pecans, toasted (see page 26)**

2 **tablespoons whole flaxseeds**

Preheat the oven to 350 degrees F. Line a rimmed baking sheet with parchment paper.

Put the squash cut-side down on the lined baking sheet and bake for 30 to 40 minutes, until soft. Let cool to room temperature. Scoop out the flesh and transfer to a blender. Add the apple juice, celery, pecans, and flaxseeds and process on high speed until smooth. Stored in a sealed container in the refrigerator, Flaxseed Dressing will keep for 12 hours (see note).

NOTE: This dressing keeps for a very short time in the refrigerator because the flaxseeds start to ferment once they are ground. To make the dressing in advance, put all the ingredients except the flaxseeds in a blender and process on high speed until smooth, then refrigerate. Just before serving, return the dressing to the blender, add the flaxseeds, and process on high speed until smooth.

Per serving (¼ cup): calories: 44.5, protein: 0.9 g, carbohydrates: 5.7 g, fat: 2.3 g, calcium: 23.6 mg, sodium: 21.4 mg, omega-3: 0.6 g

CHAPTER 7

Vegetable Dishes

VEGETABLES ARE HIGH IN NUTRIENTS AND MICRONUTRIENTS AND LOW IN CALORIES. The more vegetables you eat, the better. Dark green leafy vegetables are the most important ingredients in your diet. In fact, the best way to improve any diet is to add green leafy vegetables to it. If you think of vegetables as your nutrient foods, and fruits, grains, legumes, nuts, seeds, and avocados as your energy foods, you will be on the right track. Unsurprisingly, better ingredients lead to better results, so don't skimp when buying vegetables. Get the best that you can afford.

The recipes in this chapter can be served as side dishes, or they can play the central role in a meal. Many of them can be served hot, cold, or at room temperature.

Double Squash with Pecans and Dried Cherries

YIELD: 4 SERVINGS

THIS RECIPE COMBINES SWEET BUTTERNUT SQUASH, *pecans, and cherries with savory acorn squash, shallot, and sage. The flavors complement rather than overpower each other.*

2 butternut squash, 3 pounds each, cut lengthwise and seeds removed

2 acorn squash, 1½ pounds each, cut lengthwise and seeds removed

½ cup dried cherries

½ cup pecans, toasted (see page 26)

1 shallot, thinly sliced

10 fresh sage leaves, very thinly sliced, or ½ teaspoon dried

Preheat the oven to 350 degrees F. Line two rimmed baking sheets with parchment paper.

Put the butternut and acorn squash cut-side down on the lined baking sheets and bake the butternut squash for about 30 minutes and the acorn squash for about 20 minutes, just until tender. Let cool.

When cool enough to handle, peel and cut the squash into 1-inch cubes. Transfer to a large bowl. Add the cherries, pecans, shallot, and sage. Gently toss all the ingredients until well combined, taking care to keep the squash cubes whole. Serve at room temperature or thoroughly chilled.

NOTE: Butternut squash will generally take longer to cook than acorn squash, depending on their respective sizes. Be careful not to overcook the squash. When the squash is soft, the cubes will break apart. The flavor won't be affected, but the look and texture of the dish will.

Per serving: calories: 444.8, protein: 8.9 g, carbohydrates: 94.3 g, fat: 9.8 g, calcium: 318.1 mg, sodium: 28 mg, omega-3: 0.3 g

Sautéed Kale and Mushrooms with Ginger

YIELD: 4 SERVINGS

THERE ARE MANY VARIETIES OF VITAMIN-PACKED KALE, *which is in peak season from December to February. I like the taste of lacinato kale best, with Russian kale a close second.*

1 small yellow onion, thinly sliced

3 tablespoons peeled and chopped fresh ginger

3 cloves garlic, chopped

20 large shiitake mushrooms, stemmed and sliced

30 large lacinato kale leaves, stemmed and cut into 1-inch pieces

¼ cup vegetable broth (preferably homemade, page 28)

1 teaspoon sesame seeds, toasted (see page 26)

Put the onion, ginger, and garlic in a large dry saucepan over medium heat and cook, stirring constantly, for 3 minutes. Add the mushrooms and cook for 5 minutes, stirring occasionally. Add the kale and broth and cook for 10 minutes, stirring occasionally. Stir in the sesame seeds and cook for 2 minutes longer.

NOTE: Kale shrinks quite a bit when cooked. If only small leaves are available for purchase, buy some extra when making this recipe.

Per serving: calories: 161.9, protein: 8.8 g, carbohydrates: 33.9 g, fat: 2.1 g, calcium: 321.2 mg, sodium: 104.6 mg, omega-3: 0.4 g

Boulangère Potatoes

THIS RECIPE IS A GREAT ALTERNATIVE TO SCALLOPED POTATOES, *which are traditionally very high in fat.*

1 leek (see page 27), thinly sliced

1 yellow onion, thinly sliced

1 stalk celery, thinly sliced

2 shallots, thinly sliced

2 tablespoons chopped garlic

1 tablespoon granulated garlic

1 tablespoon granulated onion

6 cups vegetable broth (preferably homemade, page 28)

9 medium Yukon gold potatoes, peeled and very thinly sliced

1 tablespoon chopped fresh flat-leaf parsley, or 1 teaspoon dried

1 tablespoon chopped fresh thyme, or 1 teaspoon dried

Preheat the oven to 350 degrees F.

Put the leek, onion, celery, shallots, and garlic in a large dry saucepan over medium heat and cook, stirring constantly, until the onion starts to brown, about 5 minutes. Stir in the granulated garlic and granulated onion and cook for 2 minutes. Stir in the broth, increase the heat to medium-high, and simmer for 10 minutes.

Add the potatoes and stir until well combined. Decrease the heat to low and cook, stirring constantly so the potatoes don't stick together, until the potatoes are translucent, about 15 minutes. Remove from the heat and stir in the parsley and thyme.

Transfer to 13 x 9-inch baking dish and bake uncovered for about 25 minutes, until the potatoes are golden brown and fork-tender. Serve hot.

Per serving: calories: 269.3, protein: 7 g, carbohydrates: 61.5 g, fat: 0.4 g, calcium: 63.4 mg, sodium: 83.2 mg, omega-3: 0 g

Oven-Roasted Tomatoes with Arugula

SEE PHOTO ON BACK COVER

YIELD: 4 SERVINGS

ALTHOUGH ANY TOMATO WILL WORK IN THIS RECIPE, *I prefer to use Roma tomatoes. Their savory flavor is better suited to this recipe than the sweeter flavor of other tomatoes.*

12 Roma tomatoes, cut in half lengthwise

1 tablespoon granulated garlic

1 tablespoon dried onion flakes

1 tablespoon dried oregano

1 tablespoon chopped fresh basil

1 tablespoon chopped fresh chives

1 tablespoon chopped fresh flat-leaf parsley

1 tablespoon blanched fresh tarragon (see page 26), chopped

½ pound baby arugula

Preheat the oven to 250 degrees F. Line a rimmed baking sheet with parchment paper.

Put the tomatoes cut-side up on the lined baking sheet. Sprinkle with the granulated garlic, dried onion flakes, and oregano and bake for 30 minutes. Sprinkle with the basil, chives, parsley, and tarragon and bake for 5 minutes longer. Let cool. Arrange the arugula on a platter or four salad plates. Top with the tomatoes.

NOTES

- For the best results, chop the fresh herbs just before sprinkling them over the tomatoes.

- For a more refined preparation, remove the skins from the tomatoes before serving. The skins should come right off the roasted tomatoes, but be careful not to let the herbs fall off when removing the tomato skins.

Per serving: calories: 47.7, protein: 3.1 g, carbohydrates: 9.4 g, fat: 0.7 g, calcium: 109.5 mg, sodium: 24.6 mg, omega-3: 0.1 g

Grilled Ratatouille with Pesto Sauce

YIELD: 4 SERVINGS

THIS IS A VARIATION OF TRADITIONAL RATATOUILLE, *which is made with tomato sauce.*

4 large portobello mushrooms, stemmed and dark brown gills removed

3 red bell peppers, cut in half lengthwise, stemmed, and seeded

3 yellow bell peppers, cut in half lengthwise, stemmed, and seeded

3 yellow squash, sliced lengthwise ¼ inch thick

3 zucchini, sliced lengthwise ¼ inch thick

2 small eggplants, peeled and sliced ¼ inch thick

2 red onions, sliced ¼ inch thick

I cup Pesto Sauce (page 118)

Preheat the grill to medium-high. Grill the mushrooms for 5 to 7 minutes on each side. Grill the red and yellow bell peppers, yellow squash, zucchini, eggplants, and onions for 3 to 5 minutes on each side. (The cooking time will depend on how evenly your grill cooks.) Transfer the vegetables to large plates or baking sheets and let cool. When cool enough to handle, cut into bite-sized pieces. Put all the vegetables in a large bowl. Add the sauce and stir until evenly distributed.

NOTES

- Alternatively, the vegetables can be cut into bite-sized pieces and roasted. Preheat the oven to 400 degrees F. Put the vegetables on a rimmed baking sheet lined with parchment paper and roast about 10 minutes, until browned and tender.

- For a more traditional ratatouille, replace the Pesto Sauce with 2 cups of Bravo Tomato Sauce (page 117).

Per serving: calories: 242.7, protein: 11.2 g, carbohydrates: 47.7 g, fat: 3.9 g, calcium: 144.9 mg, sodium: 59.8 mg, omega-3: 0.3 g

Twice-Baked Yams and Mashed Potatoes

YIELD: 4 SERVINGS

THIS IS A FANCY WAY TO SERVE YAMS AND POTATOES. *Celery root, which can be found in most supermarkets, adds a tart and nutty flavor.*

3 medium yams, scrubbed

4 medium russet potatoes, peeled, rinsed, and cut into chunks

2 celery roots, peeled, rinsed, and cut into chunks

1 cup vegetable broth (preferably homemade, page 28)

½ cup unsweetened soymilk

½ teaspoon granulated garlic

½ teaspoon granulated onion

Preheat the oven to 350 degrees F. Line a rimmed baking sheet with parchment paper.

Put the yams on the lined baking sheet and bake for about 45 minutes, until fork-tender. Remove from the oven and let cool. Increase the oven temperature to 400 degrees F.

While the yams are baking, steam the potatoes and celery roots (see Steaming Vegetables, page 24) until soft, about 35 minutes. Transfer to a large bowl. Add the broth, soymilk, granulated garlic, and granulated onion and mash with a potato masher until all the ingredients are thoroughly incorporated and smooth. Let cool.

Put the yams in a food processor and process until smooth. Transfer to a medium bowl and let cool.

When the yams and the potato mixture are cool enough to handle, put them in separate piping bags and pipe alternating rows of yams and potatoes in a 13 x 9-inch baking dish. Bake for about 15 minutes, until the potatoes and yams are golden brown. Serve hot.

NOTES

• The yams can be baked, processed, cooled, and stored in the refrigerator for up to 2 days in advance. Unlike potatoes, yams can be piped when they are cold.

• When piping the yams and mashed potatoes, try using different pastry tips—such as one round tip and one star-shaped tip—for contrast and interest.

Per serving: calories: 515, protein: 13.3 g, carbohydrates: 115.8 g, fat: 2.1 g, calcium: 251.7 mg, sodium: 426.3 mg, omega-3: 0 g

Mustard-Braised Brussels Sprouts and Corn

YIELD: 4 SERVINGS

NOVEMBER AND DECEMBER ARE THE PEAK MONTHS FOR BRUSSELS SPROUTS. *Their flavor becomes stronger the longer they are stored, so cook them soon after purchase.*

1 small yellow onion, thinly sliced

¼ teaspoon ground toasted fennel seeds (see page 26)

¼ teaspoon granulated garlic

¼ teaspoon granulated onion

Kernels sliced from 2 ears fresh corn (see page 27), or 2 cups thawed frozen or drained canned corn

⅓ cup salt-free whole-grain mustard

Juice of ½ lemon

2 pounds Brussels sprouts, trimmed and halved

1 cup vegetable broth (preferably homemade, page 28)

2 tablespoons fresh thyme leaves, or 2 teaspoons dried

Put the onion, fennel seeds, granulated garlic, and granulated onion in a large dry saucepan over medium heat and cook for 3 minutes, stirring constantly to prevent burning. Stir in the corn, mustard, and lemon juice and cook for 30 seconds. Stir in the Brussels sprouts and broth. Decrease the heat to low, cover, and cook, stirring occasionally, for 15 minutes. Stir in the thyme and cook uncovered for 1 minute longer.

Per serving: calories: 145.1, protein: 9.4 g, carbohydrates: 30.9 g, fat: 1.2 g, calcium: 101.3 mg, sodium: 76.9 mg, omega-3: 0.2 g

Potato Wedge Salad

YIELD: 4 SERVINGS

ALTHOUGH THIS RECIPE CALLS FOR RUSSET POTATOES, *any other potato or combination of potatoes will work.*

12 medium russet potatoes, scrubbed

½ teaspoon granulated onion

Kernels sliced from 3 ears fresh corn (see page 27), or 3 cups thawed frozen or drained canned corn

1½ cups Bell Pepper Coulis (page 113)

3 green onions, sliced diagonally

1 tablespoon chopped fresh rosemary, or 1 teaspoon dried

Preheat the oven to 350 degrees F. Line a rimmed baking sheet with parchment paper.

Bake the potatoes directly on the oven rack for 40 minutes or until fork-tender. Let cool. When cool enough to handle, peel and cut each potato into 8 wedges. Arrange the potato wedges on the lined baking sheet. Sprinkle with the granulated onion and bake for 15 minutes, until golden brown.

Put the corn on a rimmed baking sheet and spread it into a single layer. Bake for 10 minutes. Transfer the corn to a large bowl. Add the potatoes, coulis, green onions, and rosemary and toss until well combined.

NOTE: The potatoes can be baked, cooled, and stored in the refrigerator for up to 2 days in advance. Just before making the salad, peel the potatoes and slice into wedges.

Per serving: calories: 601.8, protein: 17.1 g, carbohydrates: 136.7 g, fat: 1.6 g, calcium: 113.9 mg, sodium: 67.5 mg, omega-3: 0.1 g

Veggie Wraps with Herbed Hummus

YIELD: 4 WRAPS (4 SERVINGS)

THESE ROLLS MAKE A CONVENIENT MEAL FOR KIDS OR ADULTS ON THE RUN. *The combination of avocado, hummus, nuts, and vegetables is very satisfying.*

12 to 16 collard green leaves, stemmed

1 cucumber, peeled and cut into thin strips

1 red bell pepper, cut into thin strips

½ medium jicama, peeled and cut into thin strips

½ cup hearts of palm, cut into strips, rinsed, and patted dry

1 small carrot, peeled and cut into thin strips

1 stalk celery, cut into thin strips

2 cups Herbed Hummus (page 121)

1 ripe avocado, sliced

¼ cup cashews, toasted (see page 26) and slightly crushed

20 fresh basil leaves

1 tablespoon chopped fresh chives

Steam the collard green leaves (see Steaming Vegetables, page 24) for 1 minute. Remove immediately and let cool. Lay flat and arrange into four 8 x 10-inch rectangles. Lay a paper towel on top of each rectangle and roll a rolling pin over the leaves to crush the veins.

Put the cucumber, bell pepper, jicama, hearts of palm, carrot, and celery in a medium bowl and stir until well combined.

To assemble a wrap, put a rectangle of collard green leaves on a cutting board and spread one-quarter of the hummus along one of the longer edges, then arrange one-quarter of the avocado on top of the hummus and one-quarter of the cucumber mixture, cashews, basil, and chives alongside the hummus. Roll up halfway, tucking in the ends so the filling won't squeeze out. Finish by rolling the wrap as tightly as possible. Assemble the remaining wraps in the same fashion (to make 4 wraps in all).

Serve the wraps whole and eat them like burritos, or cut them into slices and serve them on a plate like sushi. Veggie Wraps with Herbed Hummus can be assembled in advance. Individually wrapped in plastic and stored in the refrigerator, they will keep for 2 days.

Per serving: calories: 373.5, protein: 12.3 g, carbohydrates: 57.6 g, fat: 12.4 g, calcium: 214.9 mg, sodium: 140.5 mg, omega-3: 0.2 g

Bravo Pizza with Polenta Crust, p. 110

Eggplant Cannelloni with Bravo Tomato Sauce, p. 102

Roasted Eggplant and Heirloom Tomatoes

YIELD: 6 SERVINGS

I USE HEIRLOOM TOMATOES IN THIS RECIPE *because they are sweeter than regular tomatoes and perfectly complement the bitterness of the eggplant. Heirloom tomatoes are in peak season from July to October.*

4 medium eggplants, peeled and cubed

2 cups sliced red onions

2 tablespoons dried oregano

1 teaspoon granulated garlic

1 cup vegetable broth (preferably homemade, page 28)

6 heirloom tomatoes, cut into bite-sized pieces

30 fresh basil leaves, sliced

Preheat the oven to 350 degrees F.

Put the eggplant in a 13 x 9-inch baking dish. Sprinkle with the red onions, oregano, and granulated garlic. Add the broth and stir until well combined. Cover with aluminum foil and bake for 30 minutes. Remove the foil and stir. Put the tomatoes on top of the eggplant and bake for 5 minutes longer. Stir until well combined, then let stand at room temperature for 1 hour to allow the eggplant to absorb the tomato juices. Add the basil and stir until evenly distributed. Serve immediately.

Per serving: calories: 131.7, protein: 5.2 g, carbohydrates: 30.7 g, fat: 0.9 g, calcium: 70.1 mg, sodium: 21.3 mg, omega-3: 0.1 g

CHAPTER 8

Bean and Grain Dishes

B EANS AND GRAINS ARE STAPLE FOODS FOR PEOPLE ALL OVER THE WORLD. They grow easily in a variety of climates, are widely available, and inexpensive. Calorie for calorie, they cost much less than fruits and vegetables while providing valuable vitamins and minerals. Eating these foods results in a satisfying fullness that promotes good health.

Separately or in combination, beans and grains provide an endless variety of textures and flavors. They also are very versatile, working equally well in cold or hot dishes.

The recipes in this chapter can be considered side dishes. However, I often pair a side dish with steamed vegetables to make a complete meal. The heartier dishes, such as the stews, are wonderful main courses.

Garbanzo Beans and Kale with Meyer Lemon and Parsley Dressing

YIELD: 6 SERVINGS

AVAILABLE OCTOBER THROUGH MAY, *Meyer lemons are sweeter and less acidic than regular lemons. Although I prefer Meyer lemons in this recipe because of their subtle flavor, regular lemons can be used instead.*

8 cups Cooked Garbanzo Beans (page 31), drained

10 lacinato kale leaves, stemmed and finely shredded

1 pint cherry tomatoes, halved

1 cup fresh cilantro leaves, firmly packed

1 cup fresh flat-leaf parsley leaves, firmly packed

Juice of 3 Meyer lemons, or 2 regular lemons

3 cloves garlic

1 shallot, peeled

1½ teaspoon cumin seeds, toasted (see page 26)

¼ cup vegetable broth (preferably homemade, page 28)

½ cup chopped fresh chives

Put the beans, kale, and tomatoes in a large bowl. Put the cilantro, parsley, lemon juice, garlic, shallot, cumin, and broth in a blender and process on high speed until smooth. Pour over the bean mixture. Add the chives and toss until well combined. Serve at room temperature or chilled.

NOTE: This dish can be prepared with hot or cold garbanzo beans.

Per serving: calories: 358.9, protein: 19.2 g, carbohydrates: 63.2 g, fat: 5.6 g, calcium: 212.3 mg, sodium: 277.3 mg, omega–3: 0.2 g

Quinoa Salad

QUINOA, WHICH ORIGINALLY COMES FROM PERU, *is technically a seed but is used like a grain. It's an excellent source of protein and is higher in unsaturated fats and lower in carbohydrates than most grains. Yellow or white varieties are common, but you can also find red and black quinoa in most natural food stores and large supermarkets. You can make this salad with just one type of quinoa or a mixture for a more dramatic effect, as I have done here. Whichever you choose, it will be equally tasty.*

1 cup white or yellow quinoa

1 cup red quinoa

5 cups vegetable broth (preferably homemade, page 28)

3 cups diced celery

1 cup diced red bell pepper

2 tablespoons blanched fresh tarragon (see page 26)

2 shallots, peeled

2 roasted red bell peppers (see page 25), cut into strips

2 roasted yellow bell peppers (see page 25), cut into strips

Kernels sliced from 2 ears fresh corn (see page 27), or 2 cups thawed frozen or drained can corn

2 teaspoons ground coriander

Put the white or yellow quinoa, the red quinoa, and 4 cups of the broth in a medium saucepan and bring to a boil over high heat. Decrease the heat to low, cover, and cook for 25 minutes. Transfer to a large bowl and let cool.

Put the remaining cup of the broth, 1 cup of the celery, the diced red bell pepper, tarragon, and shallots in a blender and process on high speed until smooth. Pour over the quinoa. Add the remaining 2 cups of the celery, the roasted red and yellow bell peppers, corn, and coriander and stir until well combined. Serve at room temperature or chilled.

Per serving: calories: 455.6, protein: 17 g, carbohydrates: 84.8 g, fat: 6.4 g, calcium: 106.7 mg, sodium: 141.5 mg, omega-3: 0.3 g

Bravo Chili

YIELD: 4 SERVINGS

CHILI IS ONE OF AMERICA'S SIGNATURE DISHES. *This nutritious version has a hearty flavor that will leave you satisfied.*

I cup dried kidney beans (see page 25), soaked in water for 8 to 12 hours

½ cup dried garbanzo beans (see page 31), soaked in water for 8 to 12 hours

½ cup dried lima beans or butter beans (see page 25), soaked in water for 8 to 12 hours

2 quarts vegetable broth (preferably homemade, page 28)

2 cups shredded cabbage

I cup diced onion

I cup peeled and diced potato

½ cup peeled and diced carrot

½ cup diced celery

½ cup diced tomatoes

3 tablespoons salt-free tomato paste

I tablespoon chopped garlic

I tablespoon dried onion flakes

I tablespoon chopped shallot

I teaspoon granulated garlic

¼ teaspoon red pepper flakes

Drain and rinse the kidney beans, garbanzo beans, and lima beans and transfer them to a large pot. Add the broth and bring to a simmer over medium-high heat. Decrease the heat to medium-low and cook uncovered, stirring occasionally, for 90 minutes, frequently using a ladle to skim off any foam that forms at the surface. Discard the foam. Stir in the cabbage, onion, potato, carrot, celery, tomatoes, tomato paste, garlic, dried onion flakes, shallot, granulated garlic, and red pepper flakes and cook uncovered, stirring occasionally, until the beans are soft, about 1 hour.

1 tablespoon chopped fresh rosemary, or 1 teaspoon dried

1 tablespoon chopped fresh sage, or 1 teaspoon dried

1 tablespoon chopped fresh thyme, or 1 teaspoon dried

Stir in the rosemary, sage, and thyme and simmer for 5 minutes longer. Serve hot. Stored in a sealed container in the refrigerator, Bravo Chili will keep for 4 days.

Per serving: calories: 408.2, protein: 23.4 g, carbohydrates: 77.3 g, fat: 2.4 g, calcium: 169.5 mg, sodium: 174.1 mg, omega-3: 0.2 g

Cannellini Bean Stew

HAVING BEEN BORN AND RAISED IN MEXICO CITY, *I was used to eating black and pink beans. In comparison, I considered white beans bland and anemic looking. However, the first time I ate white beans in the United States, I couldn't get over how well they paired with rosemary and sage. Now I always prepare white beans with these herbs.*

1½ cups dried cannellini beans (see page 25), soaked in water for 8 to 12 hours

1½ quarts vegetable broth (preferably homemade, page 28)

4 ounces sliced shiitake mushrooms

1 tablespoon chopped shallot

1 teaspoon chopped garlic

1 cup diced yellow onion

½ cup scrubbed and diced carrot

½ cup diced celery

1 teaspoon dried onion flakes

½ teaspoon granulated garlic

1 tablespoon chopped fresh rosemary, or 1 teaspoon dried

1 tablespoon chopped fresh sage, or 1 teaspoon dried

Drain and rinse the beans and transfer them to a large pot. Add the broth and bring to a simmer over medium-high heat. Decrease the heat to medium-low, cover, and cook, stirring occasionally, for 90 minutes, frequently using a ladle to skim off any foam that forms at the surface. Discard the foam.

Put the mushrooms, shallot, and garlic in a small dry saucepan over medium heat and cook, stirring frequently, for 5 minutes. Add the mushroom mixture to the beans. Stir in the onion, carrot, celery, dried onion flakes, and granulated garlic. Cover and cook, stirring occasionally, until the beans are soft, about 1 hour. Stir in the rosemary and sage. Serve hot. Stored in a sealed container in the refrigerator, Cannellini Bean Stew will keep for 4 days.

Per serving: calories: 292.9, protein: 18.8 g, carbohydrates: 55.4 g, fat: 0.8 g, calcium: 202.3 mg, sodium: 111.1 mg, omega-3: 0.1 g

Brown Lentil Stew

YIELD: 6 SERVINGS

THIS IS ONE OF THE SIMPLEST RECIPES IN THIS CHAPTER, *but it is also one of my favorites. A bowl of lentil stew, some steamed brown rice, sliced avocado, and hot sauce is a satisfying and comforting meal. If brown lentils aren't available, green lentils can be substituted.*

3 cups diced onions

2 cups diced celery

I cup scrubbed and diced carrot

I cup sliced leek (see page 27)

½ cup chopped shallots

4 quarts vegetable broth (preferably homemade, page 28)

3 cups brown lentils, rinsed and soaked in I quart vegetable broth (preferably homemade, page 28) for 2 hours

12 cloves garlic, roasted (see page 25) and chopped

I tablespoon granulated garlic

I tablespoon dried onion flakes

I tablespoon chopped fresh flat-leaf parsley, or I teaspoon dried

I tablespoon chopped fresh thyme, or I teaspoon dried

Put the onions, celery, carrot, leek, and shallots in a large dry pot over medium heat and cook, stirring occasionally, for 10 minutes. Stir in the broth and lentils, any leftover soaking liquid, and the roasted garlic. Increase the heat to medium-high and bring to a simmer. Decrease the heat to medium-low and cook uncovered, stirring occasionally, until the lentils are soft, about 1 hour, frequently using a ladle to skim off any foam that forms at the surface. Discard the foam. Stir in the granulated garlic and dried onion flakes and cook, stirring occasionally, for 30 minutes longer. Garnish with the parsley and thyme. Serve hot. Stored in a sealed container in the refrigerator, Brown Lentil Stew will keep for 4 days.

Per serving: calories: 412.5, protein: 27 g, carbohydrates: 74.5 g, fat: 1.3 g, calcium: 117.2 mg, sodium: 222.8 mg, omega-3: 0.1 g

Yellow Split Pea Stew

THIS STEW HAS A SWEET BUT SUBTLE FLAVOR. *I like to serve it with chopped green chiles sprinkled over the top to heighten the flavor.*

2 cups chopped onions

1 cup chopped celery

2 shallots, chopped

1 tablespoon chopped garlic

1½ cups yellow split peas, rinsed and soaked in 3 cups of vegetable broth (preferably homemade, page 28) for 8 to 10 hours

7 cups vegetable broth (preferably homemade, page 28)

Kernels sliced from 4 ears fresh corn (see page 27), or 2 cups thawed frozen or drained canned corn

2 cups peeled and cubed potatoes

2 cups peeled and cubed yams

1½ teaspoons granulated garlic

1½ teaspoons dried onion flakes

1 tablespoon chopped fresh parsley, or 1 teaspoon dried

1 tablespoon chopped fresh thyme, or 1 teaspoon dried

Put the onions, celery, shallots, and garlic in a large dry pot over medium heat and cook, stirring frequently, for 5 minutes. Stir in the split peas, any leftover soaking liquid, and the broth. Increase the heat to medium-high and bring to a simmer. Decrease the heat to medium-low and cook uncovered, stirring occasionally, until the split peas are almost soft, about 90 minutes, using a ladle to skim off any foam that forms at the surface. Discard the foam.

Stir in the corn, potatoes, yams, granulated garlic, and dried onion flakes. Cook uncovered, stirring occasionally, until the split peas are soft, about 30 minutes. Remove from the heat and stir in the parsley and thyme. Serve hot. Stored in a sealed container in the refrigerator, Yellow Split Pea Stew will keep for 4 days.

Per serving: calories: 535.3, protein: 25.5 g, carbohydrates: 109.7 g, fat: 2.1 g, calcium: 111.1 mg, sodium: 189.1 mg, omega-3: 0.1 g

Toasted Barley and Tomato Stew

YIELD: 6 SERVINGS

BARLEY CONTAINS GLUTEN, *so avoid this recipe if you are sensitive to gluten. I like using barley from time to time because of its robust flavor.*

1 cup hulled barley (see note)

2 cups chopped onions

1 cup chopped celery

1 cup chopped leek (see page 27)

¼ cup chopped shallots

2 tablespoons chopped garlic

2 tablespoons salt-free tomato paste

2 cups fresh or canned chopped tomatoes

2½ quarts vegetable broth (preferably homemade, page 28)

1 tablespoon dried onion flakes

2 cups coarsely chopped arugula, spinach, or watercress, firmly packed

2 tablespoons chopped fresh rosemary, or 2 teaspoons dried

2 tablespoons chopped fresh thyme, or 2 teaspoons dried

Preheat the oven to 350 degrees F.

Put the barley on a rimmed baking sheet and spread it into a single layer. Toast it in the oven for 15 minutes, stirring once or twice.

While the barley is toasting, put the onions, celery, leek, shallots, and garlic in a large dry pot over medium heat and cook, stirring occasionally, until browned, 5 to 10 minutes. Add the tomato paste and stir for 30 seconds. Stir in the tomatoes and cook for 3 minutes. Add the roasted barley and stir for 1 minute so that the barley absorbs some of the tomato flavor. Stir in the broth and dried onion flakes. Increase the heat to high and bring to a boil. Decrease the heat to medium-low and cook, stirring occasionally, until the barley is soft, about 90 minutes. Stir in the arugula, rosemary, and thyme just before serving. Serve hot.

NOTE: Pearl barley, which is more refined than hulled barley, can be used in this recipe. However, I generally avoid using pearl barley because it has been steamed and polished. The cooking time for pearl barley is about the same as for hulled barley.

Per serving: calories: 158.9, protein: 5.6 g, carbohydrates: 33.8 g, fat: 1 g, calcium: 57 mg, sodium: 111.2 mg, omega-3: 0.1 g

Red Lentil Loaf with Bell Pepper Coulis

SEE PHOTO ON BACK COVER YIELD: 4 SERVINGS

RED LENTILS ARE SMALLER THAN OTHER LENTILS AND ARE USUALLY SPLIT. *They work well for this recipe because they cook very quickly.*

1 yellow onion, diced

1 leek (see page 27), finely chopped

1 stalk celery, diced

1 shallot, diced

2 cloves garlic, chopped

1 teaspoon paprika

3 cups vegetable broth (preferably homemade, page 28)

1½ cups split red lentils

3 cups tomato purée

¾ cup yellow corn grits

½ shallot, thinly sliced

1 pound fresh spinach

1 cup Bell Pepper Coulis (page 113), heated

Put the onion, leek, celery, shallot, and garlic in a large dry saucepan over medium-high heat and cook, stirring constantly, until browned, about 5 minutes. Add the paprika and stir for 30 seconds. Stir in ¼ cup of the broth and use the spoon to loosen any bits that are stuck to the bottom of the saucepan. Add the lentils and stir for 30 seconds. Stir in the tomato purée and the remaining 2¾ cups of the broth. Bring to a simmer and cook, stirring frequently, until the lentils change from bright orange to pale orange, about 20 minutes. Stir in the corn grits, decrease the heat to low, and cook for 20 minutes, stirring frequently with a whisk to prevent lumps from forming. Pour into a loaf pan and let cool for 30 minutes. Cover and refrigerate for 8 to 10 hours, until firm.

Preheat the oven to 350 degrees F. Line a rimmed baking sheet with parchment paper.

Carefully turn the pan upside down on a cutting board and pop out the loaf. Cut the loaf into 1-inch-thick slices and arrange the slices in a single layer on the lined baking sheet. Bake for 20 minutes. If crispier slices are desired, bake for 15 minutes, turn over, and bake for 15 minutes longer.

Put the shallot in a medium dry saucepan over medium heat and cook, stirring constantly, for 2 minutes. Add the spinach and cook, stirring occasionally, until wilted, 2 to 3 minutes. Arrange the bell pepper coulis on 4 plates and top with the lentil loaf and spinach. Serve immediately.

NOTE: The lentil loaf will be somewhat soft when you cut it into slices, so handle it carefully.

Per serving: calories: 446.1, protein: 26.4 g, carbohydrates: 84.4 g, fat: 3.3 g, calcium: 200.2 mg, sodium: 167.7 mg, omega-3: 0.4 g

Blue Cornmeal Loaf

YIELD: 4 SERVINGS

HERE IS CORNBREAD WITH A TWIST. *For the best results, use fresh locally grown corn. Avoid corn that has wilted and dark silk or is sold husked or packed in trays. The kernels should be plump. Flat kernels indicate starchy corn.*

Kernels sliced from 10 ears fresh yellow corn (see page 27), or 10 cups thawed frozen or drained canned corn

2 cloves garlic

1 teaspoon ground cumin

½ teaspoon granulated garlic

Pinch cayenne

2 cups blue cornmeal

1 onion, diced

2 tablespoons chopped fresh epazote or cilantro

Preheat the oven to 400 degrees F.

Set aside 1 cup of the corn. Put the remaining corn in a large bowl. With the back of a chef's knife, scrape any pulp left on the cobs and add it to the bowl. Transfer the corn and pulp to a food processor. Add the garlic, cumin, granulated garlic, and cayenne and process until smooth. Return the mixture to the bowl. Stir in the remaining cup of corn, the cornmeal, onion, and epazote and mix thoroughly with a whisk.

Transfer to a 13 x 9-inch baking dish and bake for 20 minutes. Decrease the oven temperature to 300 degrees F, rotate the baking dish, and bake for 20 minutes longer. Let cool for 5 minutes before serving.

Per serving: calories: 325.9, protein: 10.7 g, carbohydrates: 68.8 g, fat: 4.3 g, calcium: 12.4 mg, sodium: 37 mg, omega-3: 0.1 g

Black Bean Stew

BLACK BEANS ARE MY FAVORITE, *probably because I grew up eating them in my grandmother's kitchen.*

2 cups dried black beans (see page 25), soaked in water for 8 to 12 hours

3 quarts vegetable broth (preferably homemade, page 28)

1 large onion, diced

1 carrot, scrubbed and diced

3 stalks celery, diced

2 shallots, chopped

3 cloves garlic, chopped

1 teaspoon granulated garlic

1 teaspoon dried onion flakes

1 cup fresh cilantro leaves, firmly packed, chopped

¼ cup fresh epazote leaves, lightly packed and chopped (optional)

Drain and rinse the beans and transfer them to a large pot. Add the broth and bring to a simmer over medium-high heat. Decrease the heat to medium-low, cover, and cook, stirring occasionally, for 90 minutes, frequently using a ladle to skim off any foam that forms at the surface. Discard the foam. Stir in the onion, carrot, celery, shallots, garlic, granulated garlic, and dried onion flakes. Cover and cook, stirring occasionally, until the beans are soft, about 30 minutes. Stir in the cilantro and optional epazote and simmer uncovered for 5 minutes longer. Serve hot. Stored in a sealed container in the refrigerator, Black Bean Stew will keep for 4 days.

Per serving: calories: 265.2, protein: 15.4 g, carbohydrates: 50.6 g, fat: 1 g, calcium: 110.7 mg, sodium: 131.9 mg, omega-3: 0.2 g

CHAPTER 9

Entrées

FOR THIS CHAPTER, I CHOSE POPULAR DISHES AND CREATED VEGAN VERSIONS that taste as good as—if not better than—the originals. These recipes are sure to delight you, your family, and your friends. They are easy enough to make, so you don't need to be an accomplished cook. But as any chef will tell you, difficult and intricate preparations do not guarantee a great meal. Rather, a great meal requires only that your guests enjoy what you serve. And, rest assured, they will relish these entrées.

After you've followed these recipes a few times, my guess is that you'll start creating variations of your favorites. Keep my cooking philosophy in mind: Use the finest ingredients and combine simple flavors and textures that complement each other. But let's not talk too much about philosophy now; a culinary adventure awaits you. Let's get cooking.

Forbidden Rice and Garbanzo Patties with Tomatillo Salsa

YIELD: 16 PATTIES (4 SERVINGS)

"FORBIDDEN" RICE, WHICH IS BLACK, IS MY FAVORITE VARIETY. *The name refers to the time when only emperors were allowed to eat this delicious rice. It was forbidden to everyone else.*

½ pound cremini mushrooms

3 cups Cooked Garbanzo Beans (page 31), chilled (see notes)

2 cups cooked forbidden rice (see page 25), chilled (see notes)

Kernels sliced from 2 ears fresh corn (see page 27), or 2 cups thawed frozen or drained canned corn

1 stalk celery, coarsely chopped

Juice of 1 lemon

1 shallot, coarsely chopped

2 tablespoons chopped fresh cilantro

½ teaspoon ground coriander

1 cup vegetable broth (preferably homemade, page 28)

Preheat the oven to 350 degrees F.

Put the mushrooms on a rimmed baking sheet and bake for 10 minutes. Let cool for 5 minutes, then transfer to a food processor. Add the beans, rice, corn, celery, lemon juice, shallot, cilantro, and coriander and process, slowly adding the broth until the mixture is well blended and chunky but not creamy. It should hold its shape if you roll a small portion into a ball. You may need to process the mixture in batches depending on the size of your food processor.

Line a baking sheet with parchment paper. Remove the blade from the food processor. Form the mixture into 16 equal-sized patties (use about ½ cup of the mixture for each patty) and put them on the lined baking sheet. Bake for about 15 minutes, until crisp and golden brown.

While the patties are baking, put the salsa, kale, and celery root in a large saucepan and bring to a simmer over medium-high heat. Decrease the heat to low and cook for 2 to 3 minutes. Divide the salsa mixture among four plates and top with the patties. Serve immediately.

2 cups Tomatillo Salsa (page 120)

20 kale leaves, stemmed and cut into 2-inch pieces

1 celery root, peeled and diced

NOTES

- The garbanzo beans and rice should be cold when put in the food processor, or the mixture will be too sticky.
- To form the patties, try using an ice-cream scoop to keep the shape uniform.
- For crispier patties, bake for 15 minutes, turn over, and bake for 5 minutes longer.
- It is best not to bake the patties until they are to be served. If you don't want to bake all of the patties right away, the mixture can be covered and stored in the refrigerator for up to 4 days.

Per serving (4 patties): calories: 642, protein: 29.2 g, carbohydrates: 124.9 g, fat: 8.2 g, calcium: 504.1 mg, sodium: 499.3 mg, omega-3: 0.5 g

Eggplant Cannelloni with Bravo Tomato Sauce

SEE PHOTO FACING PAGE 85 YIELD: 6 SERVINGS

CANNELLONI ARE ROUND PASTA TUBES. *In this recipe, I substitute rolled eggplant for the pasta. Select eggplants that are heavy for their size. They should have shiny, firm skins without any soft or brown spots.*

Filling

6 medium russet potatoes, peeled and cut in half widthwise

Kernels sliced from 6 ears fresh corn (see page 27), or 6 cups thawed frozen or drained canned corn

½ cup vegetable broth (preferably homemade, page 28)

½ cup unsweetened soymilk

½ teaspoon granulated garlic

½ teaspoon granulated onion

1 tablespoon blanched fresh tarragon (see page 26), chopped, or 1 teaspoon dried

Cannelloni

2 large eggplants, peeled and cut lengthwise into 1/8-inch-thick slices

½ cup vegetable broth (preferably homemade, page 28)

½ teaspoon granulated onion

4 cups Bravo Tomato Sauce (page 102)

Preheat the oven to 350 degrees F.

To make the filling, steam the potatoes (see Steaming Vegetables, page 24) until fork-tender, about 35 minutes. Transfer to a large bowl. Put half of the corn and the broth, soymilk, granulated garlic, and granulated onion in a blender and process on high speed until smooth. Spoon into the bowl with the potatoes. Add the remaining corn and the tarragon and whisk gently. (Whisking gently, rather than whipping, prevents the potatoes from getting gummy.)

To make the cannelloni, line a rimmed baking sheet with parchment paper and arrange the eggplant on it in a single layer. Brush with the broth and sprinkle with the granulated onion. Bake for 5 minutes, then turn over and bake for 3 minutes longer. Let cool. When cool enough to handle, lay on a flat surface. Spoon one-sixth of the filling on the end of one slice and roll up. Assemble 5 more rolls in the same fashion (to make 6 rolls in all). Put the rolls in a 13 x 9-inch baking dish, pour the tomato sauce over them, and bake uncovered for 15 minutes.

Topping

½ cup sliced red onion

1 teaspoon chopped garlic

1 pound fresh spinach

To make the topping, put the onion and garlic in a medium dry saucepan over medium heat and cook, stirring constantly, for 2 minutes. Add the spinach and cook, stirring occasionally, until wilted and tender, 3 to 5 minutes.

Arrange the spinach on top of the cannelloni. Serve hot or warm.

Per serving: calories: 375.6, protein: 14.3 g, carbohydrates: 83.2 g, fat: 2.6 g, calcium: 181.1 mg, sodium: 124 mg, omega-3: 0.2 g

Lasagne

IN THIS RECIPE, CASHEWS STAND IN FOR THE TRADITIONAL CHEESE. *The trick is to soak the cashews until they are very soft so that they will blend smoothly.*

2 eggplants, peeled and sliced into ½-inch-thick rounds

1 cup vegetable broth (preferably homemade, page 28)

4 sprigs rosemary, leaves removed and chopped

4 portobello mushrooms, stemmed

1 shallot, minced

4 zucchini, cut lengthwise into ⅛-inch-thick slices

1 onion, thinly sliced

2 cloves garlic, chopped

1 pound fresh spinach

1 cup raw cashews, soaked in cold water in the refrigerator for 48 hours (see notes)

8 ounces soft tofu

1½ teaspoons granulated onion

Preheat the oven to 350 degrees F.

Layer the eggplant in a 13 x 9-inch baking dish. Pour ½ cup of the broth over the top and sprinkle with the rosemary. Cover with foil and bake for 30 minutes.

Line a rimmed baking sheet with parchment paper and arrange the mushrooms on it with the gills facing up. Sprinkle with the remaining ½ cup of broth and the shallot and bake for 20 minutes. Let cool. When cool to the touch, cut the mushrooms on a diagonal into wide, thick slices.

Line a rimmed baking sheet with parchment paper, arrange the zucchini on it, and bake for 5 minutes.

Put the onion and garlic in a medium dry saucepan over medium heat and cook, stirring constantly, for 5 minutes. Add the spinach and cook, stirring occasionally, until wilted, 2 to 3 minutes. Let cool. Use your hands to squeeze all of the liquid out of the spinach mixture.

Drain the cashews and put them in a food processor. Add the tofu and granulated onion and process until smooth.

**1 package (10 ounces)
rice lasagna noodles**

**8 cups Bravo Tomato Sauce
(page 102)**

**1 cup fresh basil leaves,
firmly packed**

Layer the lasagne in a 13 x 9-inch baking pan in the following order: half of the noodles, 2 cups of the sauce, all of the mushrooms, all of the zucchini, all of the spinach mixture, another 2 cups of the sauce, the remaining noodles, another 2 cups of the sauce, all of the eggplant, all of the basil, and the remaining 2 cups of sauce. Cover with parchment paper, then with foil, and bake for about 1 hour, until the noodles are tender. Uncover, top with a single layer of the cashew mixture, and bake uncovered for 8 to 10 minutes, until the cashew mixture browns slightly.
Serve hot.

NOTES

- During the 48-hour soaking time, drain the cashews 2 or 3 times and cover them with fresh cold water.

- The eggplants, mushrooms, zucchini, and cashew mixture can be prepared 1 to 2 days in advance and stored in separate covered containers in the refrigerator.

Per serving: calories: 548.8, protein: 22.1 g, carbohydrates: 110.3 g, fat: 5 g, calcium: 341 mg, sodium: 365.2 mg, omega-3: 0.3 g

Black Bean Tamale Pie

YIELD: 6 SERVINGS

THIS RECIPE PROVIDES A GREAT WAY TO GET YOUR TAMALE FIX *without a lot of hard work.*

4 cups Tamale Dough (page 34)

6 servings Black Bean Stew (page 98)

24 green onions, trimmed

Juice of 2 limes

¼ teaspoon freshly ground pepper

2 cups Picante Salsa (page 119)

Preheat the oven to 350 degrees F.

Spread the dough evenly in a 13 x 9-inch baking dish and bake for 20 minutes. Pour off any excess liquid from the bean stew, pour the stew over the dough, and bake for 20 minutes.

While the tamale pie is baking, line a rimmed baking sheet with parchment paper. Put the green onions on the lined baking sheet and sprinkle with the lime juice and pepper.

Rotate the tamale pie and decrease the oven temperature to 300 degrees F. Put the green onions in the oven. Bake the tamale pie and the green onions for 10 minutes.

Serve the tamale pie hot, topped with the green onions and salsa.

Per serving: calories: 456.8, protein: 18.1 g, carbohydrates: 69.4 g, fat: 14.6 g, calcium: 227.3 mg, sodium: 129.1 mg, omega-3: 0.2 g

Butternut Squash and Corn Tamales

YIELD: 6 TAMALES (6 SERVINGS)

TAMALES ARE ONE OF THE MOST TRADITIONAL DISHES IN MEXICAN CUISINE.

2 butternut squash, about 3 pounds each, cut in half lengthwise and seeded

Kernels sliced from 2 ears fresh corn (see page 27), or 2 cups thawed frozen or drained canned corn

2 leeks (see page 27), thinly sliced

6 large or 12 small dried corn husks, soaked in hot water for 20 to 30 minutes (see note)

2 cups Tamale Dough (page 34)

3 cups Picante Salsa (page 119)

Preheat the oven to 350 degrees F. Line a rimmed baking sheet with parchment paper.

Put the squash skin-side up on the lined baking sheet. Bake for about 35 minutes, until fork-tender. Let cool. When cool enough to handle, scoop out the pulp and put it in a large bowl.

Put the corn and leeks in a medium dry saucepan over medium-low heat and cook, stirring constantly, for 15 minutes. Add the leeks and corn to the squash and stir until thoroughly incorporated. Let cool.

Drain the corn husks and pat them dry with paper towels. Select a large husk or overlap 2 smaller ones (totaling about 7 to 8 inches in length) and lay on a flat surface. To assemble a tamale, spread about ⅓ cup of the dough in the center of the wide end of the husk. Spread about ⅓ cup of the squash mixture on top of the dough. Wrap the husk around the filling as tightly as possible, folding down the narrow end to seal it tightly. The narrow end should be completely closed, but the other end should be left slightly open, exposing some of the filling. Assemble the remaining tamales in the same fashion (to make 6 tamales in all).

Put at least 2½ inches of water in a large pot fitted with a steamer insert. Arrange the tamales in the steamer insert with the slightly open ends up. Cover with a clean dish towel and steam for 60 minutes. Remove from the heat. Uncover and let the tamales sit for 10 minutes. Serve immediately, passing the salsa at the table.

NOTE: Before the corn husks can be used, they must be soaked. Because the husks float, you'll need to put a plate or a similar type of weight on top of them to keep them under water.

Per serving: calories: 756.3, protein: 21.8 g, carbohydrates: 120.2 g, fat: 27.3 g, calcium: 421.2 mg, sodium: 131.6 mg, omega-3: 0.3 g

Baked Tofu Stir-Fry with Sweet-and-Sour Sauce

YIELD: 4 SERVINGS

THIS GREAT STIR-FRY REQUIRES NO OIL. *If all the ingredients are served warm, the end result is wonderful.*

6 cups cooked brown rice (see page 25), completely cooled

1 package (14 ounces) firm tofu, cut into 2-inch triangles, about ½ inch thick

2 teaspoons sesame seeds

1 zucchini, cubed

1 red bell pepper, cut into 1-inch squares

1 red onion, thinly sliced

1 stalk celery, cut into 1-inch pieces

2 tablespoons peeled and chopped ginger

1 tablespoon chopped garlic

1 tablespoon chopped shallot

¼ cup vegetable broth (preferably homemade, page 28)

2 cups broccoli florets

1 cup sugar snap peas, trimmed

1⅓ cups Sweet-and-Sour Sauce (page 114)

Preheat the oven to 350 degrees F. Line two rimmed baking sheets with parchment paper.

Spread the rice on one of the lined baking sheets. Arrange the tofu on one half of the other lined baking sheet and sprinkle with the sesame seeds. Arrange the zucchini, bell pepper, onion, and celery on the other half of the baking sheet. Bake the rice, vegetables, and tofu for 10 minutes. Stir the rice. Transfer the vegetables to a covered dish to keep them warm. Bake the rice and tofu for 10 minutes longer, until the tofu is golden brown.

While the rice and tofu are baking, put the ginger, garlic, and shallot in a large dry saucepan over medium heat and cook for 3 minutes, stirring constantly. Add the broth, broccoli, and sugar snap peas and cook for 3 to 5 minutes, stirring frequently.

Put the sauce in a small saucepan and warm it over medium-low heat, stirring occasionally, until steaming, 5 to 8 minutes.

Divide the rice among four bowls. Top with the vegetables, tofu, and sauce. Serve immediately.

NOTE: Baking the rice makes this dish crunchy. Alternatively, freshly steamed rice can be used, which will make this dish smoother and softer.

Per serving: calories: 568.7, protein: 24.5 g, carbohydrates: 101 g, fat: 9.9 g, calcium: 196.2 mg, sodium: 114 mg, omega-3: 0.1 g

Tofu and Tempeh Skewers with Roasted Garlic and Tamarind Glaze

YIELD: 12 SKEWERS (6 SERVINGS)

WHO DOESN'T LOVE FOOD ON A STICK? *Better yet, who wouldn't love this healthful version? Tempeh is a high-protein soybean cake that can be found in natural food stores.*

12 large cremini mushrooms

3 packages (8 ounces each) tempeh, cut into 24 squares (see notes)

1 package (14 ounces) firm tofu, drained and cut into 24 triangles (see notes)

1 large zucchini, cut into 12 pieces

1 red bell pepper, cut into 12 pieces

1 yellow bell pepper, cut into 12 pieces

1 small red onion, cut into 12 pieces

2 cups Roasted Garlic and Tamarind Glaze (page 116)

4 cups cooked brown rice (see page 25), kept hot

Preheat the oven to 350 degrees F. Soak 12 (9-inch) skewers in water for 20 to 30 minutes.

Put the mushrooms on a rimmed baking sheet and bake for 5 minutes. Let cool. Do not turn off the oven.

Assemble the skewers so that each holds 2 pieces of tempeh, 2 pieces of tofu, 1 mushroom, and 1 piece each of zucchini, red bell pepper, yellow bell pepper, and onion. Alternate the items to create an appealing look.

Line a baking sheet with parchment paper and arrange the skewers on it. Bake for 12 minutes. Make sure the tofu triangles don't touch the edge of the baking sheet or each other, or they will stick. Brush the skewers with the glaze and bake for 3 minutes longer. Serve hot over the brown rice.

NOTES

- Baking the mushrooms makes them shrink through evaporation, which helps prevent them from falling off the skewers.

- To get 24 squares from 3 packages of tempeh, cut the contents of each package into 8 squares.

- To get 24 triangles from 1 package of tofu, cut the block of tofu into 8 triangles, then cut each triangle into 3 smaller triangles.

Per serving: calories: 398.3, protein: 18.9 g, carbohydrates: 68.2 g, fat: 7.4 g, calcium: 152.4 mg, sodium: 65.9 mg, omega–3: 0.2 g

Bravo Pizza with Polenta Crust

SEE PHOTO FACING PAGE 84   YIELD: 4 (9-INCH) PIZZAS (4 SERVINGS)

THIS FANTASTIC PIZZA IS WORTH THE TIME AND EFFORT.

Polenta Crust (page 32), chilled and cut into 4 pizza crusts

2 cups Bravo Tomato Sauce (page 102)

I zucchini, diced

I red bell pepper, diced

I small red onion, diced

I cup sliced button mushrooms

I cup fresh spinach leaves, lightly packed, shredded

I cup halved cherry tomatoes

16 fresh basil leaves

2 cloves garlic, chopped

I ½ teaspoons dried oregano

Preheat the oven to 400 degrees F. Line a baking sheet with parchment paper.

Put the crusts on the lined baking sheet and bake for 5 minutes. Carefully turn the crusts over and bake for 5 minutes longer. Spread with one-third of the sauce and bake for about 5 minutes. This process will dry out the crusts and the sauce, making the crusts crispier and giving them a more intense flavor. Spread with another third of the sauce and bake for about 5 minutes. Spread with the remaining sauce. Top with the zucchini, bell pepper, onion, mushrooms, spinach, tomatoes, basil, garlic, and oregano. Bake for 8 to 10 minutes. Serve hot.

Per serving: calories: 446.3, protein: 12.8 g, carbohydrates: 94.8 g, fat: 4.3 g, calcium: 72.1 mg, sodium: 231.3 mg, omega-3: 0.1 g

VARIATION: Once the pizza crust is ready for toppings, any combination of vegetables (such as mixed mushrooms or roasted red peppers) can be used, in addition to or instead of the ones listed in the recipe.

CHAPTER 10

Sauces and Dips

MANY OF THE SAUCES AND DIPS IN THIS CHAPTER ARE ESSENTIAL INGREDIENTS in other recipes in this book. For example, Dried Peach Sauce (page 112) tops breakfast and dessert items, Bravo Tomato Sauce (page 117) adds zing to a few entrées, and Herbed Hummus (page 121) is featured in Veggie Wraps (page 84).

The sauces also can be served over baked potatoes, quinoa, steamed rice, or vegetables. Some of them can be combined with vegetable broth and turned into a quick soup. In short, they are versatile and delicious.

In certain types of cuisine, chefs are judged in large part on the quality of their sauces. The more you can do with sauces (and dressings), the more variety you can build into your weekly and monthly menus. This chapter is the key to adding pizzazz to bean, grain, and vegetable dishes.

Dried Peach Sauce

YIELD: 1 QUART (16 SERVINGS)

THIS SAUCE IS A GREAT SUBSTITUTE FOR ANY TYPE OF SYRUP, *including agave, maple, and molasses. It's particularly good on Oatmeal "French Toast" (page 40).*

3 cups unsweetened apple juice, plus more if needed

¾ cup unsulfured dried peaches (see note)

½ teaspoon ground cinnamon

½ teaspoon ground nutmeg

Put all the ingredients in a medium saucepan, cover, and bring to a boil over high heat. Decrease the heat to low and cook for 15 minutes. Remove from the heat and let cool completely. Transfer to a blender and process on high speed until completely smooth. If the mixture is too thick to blend easily, add up to ¼ cup more apple juice, 1 tablespoon at a time. Serve hot or cold. Stored in a sealed container in the refrigerator, Dried Peach Sauce will keep for 10 days.

NOTE: When you purchase dried fruit, make sure it is unsulfured. Sulfur is added to dried fruit to make the color more vibrant. Unsulfured fruit, although not as bright in color, tastes better and doesn't create health risks. Sulfured fruit can cause allergic reactions or asthma attacks, especially in children.

Per serving (¼ cup): calories: 39.3, protein: 0.3 g, carbohydrates: 9.9 g, fat: 0.1 g, calcium: 5.8 mg, sodium: 2.4 mg, omega-3: 0 g

VARIATION: Replace the dried peaches with unsulfured dried apricots or dried nectarines.

Bell Pepper Coulis

YIELD: I QUART (16 SERVINGS)

THIS SAUCE IS TRADITIONALLY MADE WITH OLIVE OIL, *but the flavor is superb even without it. Try serving Bell Pepper Coulis hot over steamed vegetables, as a hot or cold soup, or even as a cold dip for slices of baked potato.*

4 cups cubed red or yellow bell peppers (about 5 peppers)

1½ cups vegetable broth (preferably homemade, page 28)

1 leek (see page 27), sliced

1 small bulb fennel, coarsely chopped

1 small yellow onion, coarsely chopped

1 stalk celery, sliced

1 shallot, coarsely chopped

1 clove garlic, coarsely chopped

5 sprigs basil

5 sprigs thyme

Put the bell peppers and 1¼ cups of the broth in a blender and process on high speed until smooth. Set aside.

Put the leek, fennel, onion, celery, shallot, garlic, and the remaining ¼ cup of the broth in a medium saucepan over medium heat and cook, stirring frequently, for 5 minutes, being careful not to brown the vegetables. Stir in the bell pepper mixture. Increase the heat to medium-high and simmer for 10 minutes. Add the basil and thyme to one side of the saucepan (for easier removal later), decrease the heat to medium-low, and cook for 5 minutes longer. Remove and discard the basil and thyme. Transfer to a blender and process on high speed until smooth. Strain through a fine-mesh strainer. Stored in a sealed container in the refrigerator, Bell Pepper Coulis will keep for 5 days.

Per serving (¼ cup): calories: 24.2, protein: 0.7 g, carbohydrates: 5.2 g, fat: 0.2 g, calcium: 15.9 mg, sodium: 16.7 mg, omega-3: 0 g

Sweet-and-Sour Sauce

YIELD: 1 QUART (12 SERVINGS)

THIS RECIPE OUTPERFORMS ITS TRADITIONAL COUNTERPART *in both flavor and texture. It goes well with Baked Tofu Stir-Fry (page 108) and also pairs wonderfully with steamed vegetables.*

1 red bell pepper, diced

1 cup vegetable broth (preferably homemade, page 28)

1 leek (see page 27), diced

1 yellow onion, diced

1 stalk celery, diced

1 shallot, diced

1 tablespoon peeled and chopped fresh ginger

2 cloves garlic, chopped

2 tablespoons rice flour

1 cup unsweetened pineapple juice

Put the bell pepper and broth in a small food processor or blender and process until smooth. Set aside.

Put the leek, onion, celery, shallot, ginger, and garlic in a medium saucepan over medium heat and cook, stirring frequently, until the vegetables start to brown, 4 to 5 minutes. Add the rice flour and stir for 30 seconds. Stir in the bell pepper mixture and pineapple juice and cook, stirring frequently, for 15 minutes. Transfer to a blender and process on high speed until smooth. Strain through a fine-mesh strainer. Pour into a clean medium saucepan (or rinse out the one used earlier) and reheat over medium-low heat until steaming. Serve hot. Stored in a sealed container in the refrigerator, Sweet-and-Sour Sauce will keep for 1 week.

NOTE: If the leek mixture starts to burn, stir in 2 tablespoons of broth.

Per serving (⅓ cup): calories: 34.1, protein: 0.6 g, carbohydrates: 7.8 g, fat: 0.2 g, calcium: 14.9 mg, sodium: 11.5 mg, omega-3: 0 g

Saffron-Tomato Compote

YIELD: 1 QUART (4 SERVINGS)

THIS IS THE ONLY SAUCE RECIPE IN THIS CHAPTER *that wasn't specifically created to go with another recipe in this book. I decided to include it because Saffron-Tomato Compote is terrific over baked potatoes, quinoa, or steamed rice. The roasted garlic is rich and pungent yet sweet and savory at the same time.*

1 ½ cups diced onions

1 cup diced celery

1 tablespoon diced shallot

Pinch saffron threads

6 cups seeded and diced fresh or canned tomatoes

20 cloves garlic, roasted (see page 25)

¼ cup chopped chives

Put the onions, celery, shallot, and saffron in a medium dry saucepan over medium heat and cook, stirring occasionally, until the bottom of the saucepan is well browned, 4 to 5 minutes. Add the tomatoes and simmer, stirring occasionally, until the volume is reduced by half, 15 to 20 minutes. Stir in the garlic and cook for 2 minutes. Remove from the heat and let cool for 30 minutes. Stir in the chives just before serving. Stored in a sealed container in the refrigerator, Saffron-Tomato Compote will keep for 5 days.

Per serving (1 cup): calories: 93.5, protein: 3.9 g, carbohydrates: 20.7 g, fat: 0.7 g, calcium: 71.4 mg, sodium: 38.1 mg, omega-3: 0 g

Roasted Garlic and Tamarind Glaze

YIELD: 2 CUPS (6 SERVINGS)

TAMARIND CAN BE FOUND IN MANY DIFFERENT FORMS IN ASIAN MARKETS. *It is relatively inexpensive and has a long shelf life. I use tamarind pulp, which comes in small blocks and has only one ingredient: tamarind. Whether served hot or cold, this glaze works great as a dip for steamed or raw vegetables.*

1 cup tamarind pulp, cut into small pieces

1½ cups vegetable broth (preferably homemade, page 28), plus more if needed

1 leek (see page 27), diced

1 yellow onion, chopped

1 stalk celery, chopped

1 shallot, chopped

15 cloves garlic, roasted (see page 25)

1 tablespoon raisins

1 teaspoon celery seeds

1 teaspoon granulated garlic

1 teaspoon dried onion flakes

Preheat the oven to 350 degrees F.

Put the tamarind pulp and ½ cup of the broth in a small saucepan. Cover and cook over low heat until the pulp is soft, 12 to 15 minutes. Strain through a fine-mesh strainer to remove the tamarind seeds and fiber. Set aside.

Put the leek, onion, celery, and shallot in a medium dry saucepan. Cover and cook over medium heat, stirring occasionally, for 5 minutes. Stir in the roasted garlic, raisins, celery seeds, granulated garlic, and dried onion flakes and cook for about 1 minute. Add the remaining cup of the broth and simmer until the liquid is reduced by half, about 5 minutes. Stir in the tamarind mixture and cook for 5 minutes longer. Transfer to a food processor and process until smooth. If the mixture is too thick, add more broth, 1 tablespoon at a time, until the desired consistency is achieved. Stored in a sealed container in the refrigerator, Roasted Garlic and Tamarind Glaze will keep for 2 weeks.

NOTE: Tamarind pulp will always need to be strained, even if it's labeled seedless. There are always seeds and bits of fiber in it.

Per serving (⅓ cup): calories: 93, protein: 2 g, carbohydrates: 23 g, fat: .02 g, calcium: 49 mg, sodium: 25.5 mg, omega-3: 0 g

Peach-Blueberry Crisp, p. 127

Mango-Banana Pie, p. 129

Bravo Tomato Sauce

YIELD: 2 QUARTS (16 SERVINGS)

THE COMBINATION OF FRESH AND PACKAGED TOMATOES *gives this sauce the right flavor and consistency. If only fresh tomatoes are used, the sauce does not become thick enough.*

1½ pounds Roma tomatoes

1 large yellow onion, diced

1 stalk celery, diced

1 shallot, diced

4 cloves garlic, diced

1 tablespoon dried oregano

1 teaspoon granulated garlic

1 teaspoon dried onion flakes

¼ teaspoon red pepper flakes (optional)

¼ cup vegetable broth (preferably homemade, page 28)

3 cups chopped tomatoes, canned or packaged

½ cup fresh basil leaves, firmly packed and chopped

Put the Roma tomatoes in a blender and process on high speed until smooth. Pour through a strainer to remove the seeds and skins. Set aside.

Put the onion, celery, shallot, and garlic in a large dry saucepan over medium-high heat and cook, stirring occasionally, until the vegetables and the bottom of the saucepan are browned, about 5 minutes. Add the oregano, granulated garlic, dried onion flakes, and optional red pepper flakes and cook, stirring almost constantly, for 1 minute. Stir in the broth and cook until the bottom of the saucepan is dry and browned, 5 to 10 minutes. Stir in the chopped tomatoes and strained Roma tomatoes and bring to a simmer. Decrease the heat to medium and cook for 15 minutes. Stir in the basil. Serve hot. Stored in a sealed container, Bravo Tomato Sauce will keep for 1 week in the refrigerator.

NOTES

• The yield for Bravo Tomato Sauce is double that of all the other sauces in this book because it is used in so many recipes. I recommend always having some on hand.

• Depending on your preference, the sauce can be left chunky or processed in batches in a blender until smooth.

Per serving (½ cup): calories: 25.5, protein: 1 g, carbohydrates: 5.7 g, fat: 0.2 g, calcium: 16.9 mg, sodium: 9.7 mg, omega-3: 0 g

Pesto Sauce

YIELD: 2 CUPS (4 SERVINGS)

RATHER THAN TRYING TO SUBSTITUTE OTHER INGREDIENTS *for the cheese and oil in a traditional pesto, I just omit them and let the flavors of the basil, garlic, and pine nuts flourish unmasked. This sauce is great served over sliced raw tomatoes and onions or mixed into steamed rice.*

2 cups fresh basil leaves, firmly packed, blanched (see page 26), and chopped

½ cup fresh spinach, firmly packed

½ cup vegetable broth (preferably homemade, page 28)

3 cloves garlic

3 tablespoons pine nuts, toasted (see page 26)

Put all the ingredients in a blender and process on high speed until smooth. Stored in a sealed container in the refrigerator, Pesto Sauce will keep for 3 days.

NOTES

• For the best results, use the freshest and greenest basil available.

• The yield for this recipe may seem small, but a little bit goes a long way.

Per serving (½ cup): calories: 54.8, protein: 2.4 g, carbohydrates: 2.5 g, fat: 4.6 g, calcium: 71.8 mg, sodium: 29.9 mg, omega-3: 0.1 g

Picante Salsa

YIELD: 1 QUART (4 SERVINGS)

THIS IS A VERY EASY SALSA TO MAKE. *The dried chiles can be found at any Latin market and in the ethnic section of many large supermarkets.*

10 Roma tomatoes, halved

½ cup sliced red onion

1 tablespoon chopped garlic

½ fresh ancho chile, seeded (see note)

2 dried red chiles, soaked in water for 5 minutes, drained, and seeded (see note)

15 sprigs cilantro, with stems

Preheat the oven to 350 degrees F. Line a rimmed baking sheet with parchment paper.

Put the tomatoes skin-side down on the lined baking sheet. Sprinkle the onion and garlic over the tomatoes and bake for 15 minutes. Let cool.

Put the tomatoes, including the onion and garlic, ancho and red chiles, and cilantro in a blender and process on high speed until smooth. Stored in a sealed container in the refrigerator, Picante Salsa will keep for 5 days.

NOTE: I recommend wearing rubber gloves when seeding hot chiles. For a spicier salsa, leave the seeds in the chiles.

Per serving (1 cup): calories: 69, protein: 3.1 g, carbohydrates: 15.3 g, fat: 0.7 g, calcium: 39.3 mg, sodium: 18.8 mg, omega-3: 0 g

Tomatillo Salsa

YIELD: 1 QUART (4 SERVINGS)

TOMATILLOS CAN BE FOUND IN LATIN MARKETS YEAR-ROUND. *Choose plump tomatillos with no soft spots. Bright green tomatillos will be tangier than the more yellow ones.*

2 green onions, trimmed and thinly sliced

1½ pounds green tomatillos, husks removed, rinsed, and halved

1 green bell pepper, roasted (see page 25)

1 small white onion, diced

¼ cup chopped fresh cilantro

1 jalapeño chile (optional)

1 clove garlic

½ teaspoon ground coriander

½ teaspoon ground cumin

Put half of the green onions and the tomatillos, bell pepper, onion, cilantro, optional chile, garlic, coriander, and cumin in a food processor and process until the desired consistency is achieved. Garnish with the remaining green onions. Stored in a sealed container in the refrigerator, Tomatillo Salsa will keep for 3 days.

NOTE: Add more jalapeños if a spicier salsa is desired.

Per serving (1 cup): calories: 42.1, protein: 1.3 g, carbohydrates: 8.4 g, fat: 0.9 g, calcium: 16.9 mg, sodium: 4.1 mg, omega-3: 0 g

ROASTED TOMATILLO SALSA: Preheat the oven to 350 degrees F. Line a rimmed baking sheet with parchment paper. Put the tomatillos, onion, chile, and garlic on the lined baking sheet and roast for 15 minutes before processing. Note that the yield will be lower because the tomatillos will lose moisture during the roasting process.

Herbed Hummus

YIELD: 1 QUART (8 SERVINGS)

THIS DELICIOUS DIP IS MUCH LOWER IN FAT THAN TRADITIONAL HUMMUS. *Enjoy it inside Veggie Wraps (page 84), as a complement to raw vegetable sticks, or as a topping for baked potatoes.*

1 cup fresh basil leaves, lightly packed and blanched (see page 26)

½ cup fresh tarragon leaves, lightly packed and blanched (see page 26)

4 cups Cooked Garbanzo Beans (page 31)

1 cup vegetable broth (preferably homemade, page 28)

½ cup fresh flat-leaf parsley leaves, lightly packed

Juice of 1 lemon

2 tablespoons sesame seeds, toasted (see page 26)

2 cloves garlic

¼ cup chopped chives (see note)

Pat the basil and tarragon dry and coarsely chop them. Transfer to a food processor. Add the beans, broth, parsley, lemon juice, sesame seeds, and garlic and process until the desired consistency is achieved. Stir in the chives. Stored in a sealed container in the refrigerator, Herbed Hummus will keep for 4 days.

NOTE: Most food processors don't do a good job of chopping chives, as the chives tend to get wound around the base of the blade. That's why I suggest that you chop them by hand.

Per serving (½ cup): calories: 119.8, protein: 6.1 g, carbohydrates: 18.7 g, fat: 2.7 g, calcium: 50.1 mg, sodium: 93.7 mg, omega-3: 0 g

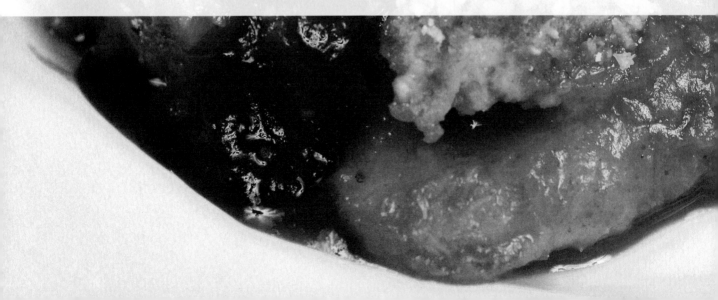

CHAPTER 11

Desserts

I MEET MANY PEOPLE WHO THINK THAT DESSERT MADE WITHOUT REFINED SUGAR ISN'T REALLY DESSERT. The poor dears don't know what they're missing. The only requirement that I know of for dessert is that it tastes sweet and delicious, and the following recipes meet these criteria.

Desserts made with healthful ingredients can be just as satisfying as those that run up your dental bills. Crisps, cobblers, fruit and nut bars, pies, and puddings are among the delectable treats you'll find in this chapter. Here's the best part: Unlike with sugary, fat-laden desserts, you don't have to limit yourself to tiny portions. These desserts are good for you. They can also be varied endlessly, so experiment and invent some that are all your own.

Apple-Strawberry Gelée

AGAR, WHICH IS DERIVED FROM SEA VEGETABLES, *is an excellent substitute for gelatin, which is derived from animals. Agar flakes can be found in Asian markets, natural food stores, and specialty food stores.*

4 cups unsweetened apple juice

4 tablespoons agar flakes

½ pound strawberries, hulled and diced

¼ cup unsweetened applesauce

Put the apple juice and agar flakes in a medium saucepan over medium-low heat and cook, stirring occasionally, for 15 minutes, until the agar flakes dissolve and the mixture starts to thicken. Stir in the strawberries and applesauce. Pour into four small dishes and let cool for 30 minutes. Cover and refrigerate for at least 4 hours before serving. Serve chilled. Covered and stored in the refrigerator, Apple-Strawberry Gelée will keep for 3 to 4 days.

Per serving: calories: 142.5, protein: 0.7 g, carbohydrates: 35 g, fat: 0.5 g, calcium: 31.4 mg, sodium: 10.9 mg, omega-3: 0.1 g

Orange-Cinnamon Rice Pudding

WHEN I WAS A KID, I LOVED IT WHEN MY GRANDMOTHER COOKED ARROZ CON LECHE. *Leche is Spanish for "milk," and milk, of course, is not used in vegan cuisine. In this recipe, soymilk serves as a healthful substitution. It combines with the starch from the rice and the sugar from the apple juice to create a creamy, sweet pudding.*

4 cups unsweetened apple juice

I cup short-grain brown rice

Zest and juice from I orange

¼ cup raisins

I teaspoon ground cinnamon

I teaspoon peeled and chopped fresh ginger

½ vanilla bean, split lengthwise, or ½ teaspoon alcohol-free vanilla extract

2 cups unsweetened soymilk

¼ cup almonds, toasted (see page 26) and crushed

Put the apple juice, rice, orange zest and juice, raisins, cinnamon, ginger, and vanilla bean in a medium saucepan and stir to combine. Bring to a boil over high heat. Cover, decrease the heat to low, and cook for 1 hour. Stir in the soymilk and almonds. Remove the vanilla bean, scrape the seeds back into the saucepan, and discard the bean. Increase the heat to medium-low and cook uncovered, stirring occasionally, until starting to bubble. Let cool for 1 hour at room temperature. Cover and refrigerate for 8 hours before serving. Serve chilled. Covered and stored in the refrigerator, Orange-Cinnamon Rice Pudding will keep for 5 days.

NOTE: Don't be alarmed if the rice pudding looks runny before it is refrigerated. As it chills, the rice will absorb the excess liquid.

Per serving: calories: 430, protein: 9.8 g, carbohydrates: 81.2 g, fat: 8.1 g, calcium: 226.3 mg, sodium: 72.5 mg, omega-3: 0 g

Fig-Pecan Bars

YIELD: 6 SERVINGS

THESE ARE THE BEST FIG BARS YOU CAN IMAGINE, *and they don't contain the unhealthful ingredients found in most commercial bars.*

2 cups dried figs

2 cups unsweetened pineapple juice

I vanilla bean, sliced in half lengthwise, or I teaspoon alcohol-free vanilla extract

4 cups Nutty Dough (page 35)

Put the figs, pineapple juice, and vanilla bean in a medium saucepan over medium-low heat and cook, stirring occasionally, for 15 minutes. Decrease the heat to low and cook until the figs are soft, about 5 minutes. Remove the vanilla bean, scrape the seeds back into the saucepan, and discard the bean. Let cool for 20 minutes. Transfer to a food processor and process until smooth.

Preheat the oven to 350 degrees F. Line a baking sheet with parchment paper.

Put half of the dough on the lined baking sheet and put a piece of parchment paper on top. Use a rolling pin to roll out the dough until it is about ⅛ inch thick. Remove and set aside. Roll out the remaining half of the dough in the same fashion until it is the same size and shape as the first half. Put both pieces of dough on the lined baking sheet and bake for 10 minutes to make two crusts. Let cool for 10 minutes.

Spread the fig mixture in a single layer on one of the crusts. Carefully position the other crust on top of the fig mixture. Bake until the top crust is well browned, about 15 minutes. Let cool for at least 2 hours before cutting into 2-inch pieces. Covered and stored in the refrigerator, Fig-Pecan Bars will keep for 1 week.

NOTE: If you put the cooled top crust in the freezer for 10 minutes before putting it on top of the fig mixture, it will be easier to handle and less likely to break.

Per serving: calories: 523.7, protein: 10.3 g, carbohydrates: 71.7 g, fat: 24.3 g, calcium: 115.6 mg, sodium: 11.6 mg, omega-3: 0.2 g

Peach-Blueberry Crisp

SEE PHOTO FACING PAGE 116

YIELD: 6 SERVINGS

FOR THIS RECIPE TO WORK PROPERLY, THE PEACHES MUST BE FULLY RIPE *and the berries must be at their peak of flavor. This is the perfect dessert for spring and summer.*

12 ripe peaches, unpeeled and cubed

1 teaspoon ground cinnamon

½ teaspoon ground nutmeg

12 ounces fresh blueberries (about 1½ cups)

½ cup Dried Peach Sauce (page 112)

2 cups Nutty Dough (page 35)

Preheat the oven to 350 degrees F.

Put the peaches, cinnamon, and nutmeg in a medium saucepan over high heat and cook for 5 minutes, stirring constantly. Add the blueberries and cook, stirring occasionally, for 2 minutes. Put a strainer over a medium bowl and pour the mixture through the strainer to separate the fruit from the juice. Return the juice to the saucepan. Transfer the fruit to a 13 x 9-inch baking dish. Add the Dried Peach Sauce to the juice and cook, stirring occasionally, over medium-low heat until syrupy, about 5 minutes. Pour over the fruit. Roll the dough between two pieces of plastic wrap into a rectangle about 13 x 9 inches, and carefully position it on top of the fruit. Bake for 20 minutes, until well browned. Let cool slightly before serving. Covered and stored in the refrigerator, Peach-Blueberry Crisp will keep for 4 days.

Per serving: calories: 394.7, protein: 9.2 g, carbohydrates: 58 g, fat: 16.9 g, calcium: 63.4 mg, sodium: 7.5 mg, omega-3: 0.1 g

Apple-Pecan Cobbler

YIELD: 4 SERVINGS

UNLIKE A CRISP, THIS COBBLER HAS A FLUFFY, SPONGY TOPPING. *The texture is similar to that of an apple muffin.*

Filling

12 large Gala or Fuji apples, peeled and cut into large slices (about 6 slices per apple)

½ teaspoon ground nutmeg

Zest and juice of 1 orange

¾ cup Dried Peach Sauce (page 112)

Topping

2 cups oat flour

1 teaspoon baking powder

1 teaspoon ground cinnamon

½ teaspoon ground nutmeg

1½ cups unsweetened soymilk

1 cup unsweetened applesauce

¾ cup Coconut-Vanilla Granola (page 36)

½ cup pecans

Preheat the oven to 350 degrees F. Line a rimmed baking sheet with parchment paper.

To make the filling, arrange the apples in a single layer on the lined baking sheet and sprinkle with the nutmeg. Bake for 15 minutes, just until starting to soften. Heat a large dry skillet over medium-high heat for 2 minutes. Put the apples in the skillet (if the apples don't sizzle immediately, the skillet isn't hot enough). Cook, stirring constantly, for 1 minute. Stir in the zest and the peach sauce and continue stirring until the apples caramelize, about 1 minute. Stir in the orange juice and cook for 10 seconds longer. Transfer the filling to a 13 x 9-inch baking pan.

To make the topping, put the flour, baking powder, cinnamon, and nutmeg in a medium bowl and stir with a dry whisk to combine. Put the soymilk and applesauce in a small bowl and stir until combined. Pour into the flour mixture and whisk for 1 minute. Stir in the granola until well incorporated.

To assemble the cobbler, spoon the topping in a single layer over the filling. Bake for 15 minutes. Remove from the oven and randomly insert the pecans into the cobbler. Return to the oven and bake for about 10 minutes longer, until golden brown. Cool slightly before serving. Serve warm or chilled. Covered and stored in the refrigerator, Apple-Pecan Cobbler will keep for 4 days.

NOTE: You may need to cook the apples in batches depending on the size of your skillet. Either use more than one skillet or clean the skillet and repeat the process until all the apples are ready for the filling.

Per serving: calories: 741, protein: 14.4 g, carbohydrates: 143.2 g, fat: 16.7 g, calcium: 183.9 mg, sodium: 51.7 mg, omega-3: 0.2 g

Mango-Banana Pie ⚡ ⚡ ⚡ ⚡ ⚡ ⚡ ⚡ ⚡ ⚡ ⚡ ⚡ ⚡

SEE PHOTO FACING PAGE 117   YIELD: 6 SERVINGS

MANGOES ARE AVAILABLE YEAR–ROUND, *so you can enjoy this refreshing dessert any time.*

Crust

½ cup Coconut-Vanilla Granola (page 36)

6 soft dates, pitted

Filling

2 cups unsweetened pineapple juice

1 tablespoon agar flakes

½ vanilla bean, sliced lengthwise, or 1 teaspoon alcohol-free vanilla extract

2 ripe mangoes, cubed, or 3 cups frozen mango chunks

3 ripe bananas, cut into ½-inch pieces

2 cups unsweetened shredded dried coconut

To make the crust, put the granola and dates in a food processor and pulse until a sticky paste forms. Press evenly into a 9-inch pie plate and set aside.

To make the filling, put the pineapple juice, agar flakes, and vanilla bean in a medium saucepan over medium-high heat and bring to a simmer. Decrease the heat to low, cover, and cook for 12 minutes, until the agar flakes dissolve and the mixture starts to thicken. Remove the vanilla bean, scrape the seeds back into the saucepan, and discard the bean. Increase the heat to medium, stir in the mangoes and bananas, and cook, stirring occasionally, until the bananas start to look translucent, about 5 minutes. Scoop out about 90 percent of the fruit with a strainer and transfer it to the pie plate, leaving the juice and a bit of fruit behind. Let cool for at least 10 minutes.

Preheat the oven to 350 degrees F.

Spread 2 teaspoons of the coconut in a single layer on a baking sheet and bake for 2 minutes, until lightly toasted. Put the remaining coconut, the juice, and the remaining fruit in a food processor and process until smooth. Spoon evenly over the fruit mixture in the crust. Sprinkle with the toasted coconut and refrigerate for at least 1 hour before serving. Covered and stored in the refrigerator, Mango-Banana Pie will keep for 4 days.

Per serving: calories: 457.7, protein: 4.9 g, carbohydrates: 67.6 g, fat: 22.4 g, calcium: 49.2 mg, sodium: 16.8 mg, omega-3: 0.1 g

Sweet Yam Pie

YIELD: 6 SERVINGS

THIS IS A GREAT ALTERNATIVE TO PUMPKIN PIE.

1 ½ cups **Nutty Dough (page 35)**

2 medium yams, scrubbed

1 ½ cups **unsweetened apple juice**

4 teaspoons agar flakes

1 ½ teaspoons **pumpkin pie spice**

1 ½ teaspoons **raisins**

½ **vanilla bean, sliced in half lengthwise, or** 1 **teaspoon alcohol-free vanilla extract**

¾ cup **unsweetened soymilk**

Preheat the oven to 350 degrees F. Line a rimmed baking sheet with parchment paper.

Press the dough evenly in a 9-inch pie plate and bake about 10 minutes, until golden brown. The pie plate may need to be rotated in the oven for even baking. Let cool.

Put the yams on the lined baking sheet and bake about 40 minutes, until soft. Let cool. When cool enough to handle, peel the yams, put them in a food processor, and process until smooth. Set aside.

Put the apple juice, agar flakes, pumpkin pie spice, raisins, and vanilla bean in a medium saucepan and bring to a simmer over medium-low heat. Cook until the liquid is reduced by half, 10 to 12 minutes. Decrease the heat to low and stir in the soymilk. Remove the vanilla bean, scrape the seeds back into the saucepan, and discard the bean. Scoop out and discard the raisins. Add the yams and stir until thoroughly incorporated.

Transfer to a food processor and process until smooth. Pour into the cooled pie shell. Lift the pie plate and tap it lightly against a counter or cutting board to force any air bubbles out of the filling. Let cool for 30 minutes, then refrigerate uncovered for at least 2 hours before slicing. Serve chilled. Covered and stored in the refrigerator, Sweet Yam Pie will keep for 5 days.

NOTE: The yams can be baked up to 2 days in advance and refrigerated. If you prepare the yams in advance, warm them briefly on the stovetop before proceeding with the recipe. Two medium yams will yield about 1 ½ cups mashed.

Per serving: calories: 278.3, protein: 5.9 g, carbohydrates: 37 g, fat: 12.6 g, calcium: 70.9 mg, sodium: 26.3 mg, omega-3: 0.1 g

Glossary

Agar flakes. Agar is a tasteless sea vegetable that acts as a setting or gelling agent. It is a substitute for gelatin, which is made from animal products. Agar is sold in various forms, including flakes.

Blood orange. Blood oranges are sweet-and-tart oranges with red or red-streaked white flesh.

Blue cornmeal. Blue cornmeal is made from dried and finely ground kernels of naturally blue corn.

Celery root. Also known as celeriac, celery root is a type of celery that is cultivated specifically for its root. This rather ugly, knobby brown vegetable tastes like a cross between celery and parsley. Celery root can be eaten raw or cooked.

Chayote. Chayotes are gourdlike fruits that are about the size and shape of a large pear. They have pale green skin, white flesh, and a soft seed.

Chioggia beet. Also called candy cane beets, chioggia beets have deep pink flesh with white rings. They do not "bleed" like red beets do.

Corn husks. The dry, papery husks from corn are used primarily in the making of tamales. They must be soaked in hot water and softened before they can be used.

Curry powder. Used primarily in Indian cuisine, curry powder is a blend of pulverized herbs, seeds, and spices.

Enoki mushroom. Enoki are crisp, delicate mushrooms that have long, thin stems topped with tiny snow-white caps.

Epazote. A pungent wild herb, epazote has flat, pointed leaves and a strong flavor. Look for fresh epazote in Latin markets. It is sometimes available in dried form in specialty stores. Use one teaspoon of dried epazote to replace one tablespoon of fresh.

Fennel. Fennel is a vegetable with a broad, bulbous base. Both the base and the stems can be eaten raw or cooked.

Flaxseeds. Flaxseeds are high in essential nutrients, including calcium, iron, niacin, omega-3 fatty acids, phosphorous, and vitamin E. Considered a digestive aid, flaxseeds also have laxative effects.

Forbidden rice. Forbidden rice is a medium-sized heirloom rice characterized by its deep purple to black color. The name refers to ancient times, when only emperors were allowed to eat it.

Galangal. Galangal is a root with creamy white flesh and a hot, gingery-peppery flavor.

Ginger. Ginger is a root with a peppery, slightly sweet flavor and a pungent, spicy aroma.

Hearts of palm. Grown in many tropical climates, hearts of palm are the edible inner portions of the stems of the cabbage palm tree.

Heirloom tomato. Heirloom tomatoes are varieties of extremely flavorful tomatoes characterized by brilliant multicolored skin and flesh. Their peak season is from June to September.

Jicama. Native to Central America and used in Mexican cuisine, jicama is a large bulbous root vegetable with a thin brown skin and white, crunchy flesh.

Kabocha squash. Kobocha is a winter squash with a green rind and pale orange flesh.

Kaffir lime leaf. Used primarily in Indonesian and Thai cooking, kaffir lime leaves are dark green and have an intense citrus aroma.

Kelp noodles. Made from a sea vegetable, kelp noodles are clear and glossy, crunchy, and slightly salty.

Kombu. Kombu is a dark brown to grayish-black sea vegetable.

Lemongrass. Lemongrass is an herb with long, thin, yellow-green leaves and a woody base. It has a lemony flavor and fragrance.

Masa harina. Made from corn treated with lime water, masa harina is the traditional corn flour used for making corn tortillas and tamales.

Meyer lemon. A cross between a lemon and an orange, Meyer lemons are sweeter and less acidic than regular lemons.

Nori. Nori is a sea vegetable with a sweet ocean taste. It is sold in paper-thin dried sheets.

Persimmon. Persimmons are winter fruits that have glossy orange skin and sweet orange flesh. The two most common types are fuyu, which has a firmer flesh, and hachiya, which has a jellylike flesh when fully ripe.

Plantain. A very large and firm variety of banana, plantains are typically cooked, even when green. However, they can be eaten raw if fully ripe.

Polenta. A mush made from cornmeal, polenta can be eaten hot and freshly cooked or allowed to cool until firm, then cut and cooked again.

Pomegranate. Pomegranates are fruits with leathery skin. The interior houses hundreds of deep red seeds that are separated by bitter, cream-colored membranes.

Saffron. The most expensive spice in the world, saffron is made from the yellow-orange stigmas of a small purple crocus. Saffron is pungent and aromatic and infuses food with a bright yellow color.

Sunchoke. Sunchokes are lumpy, brown-skinned tubers that slightly resemble ginger. They have a pronounced sweet and nutty flavor.

Tahini. Tahini is a thick paste made from ground sesame seeds.

Tamale. In Mexican cuisine, tamales are made by wrapping corn flour dough and other fillings inside of corn husks.

Tamarind pulp. Tamarind pulp is made from the fruit pod of a small shade tree native to Asia. It has a sweet-and-sour flavor reminiscent of apricots and lemons.

Tempeh. Originating in Indonesia, tempeh is a firm, dense, hearty food made from fermented cooked soybeans.

Tofu. Also known as bean curd, tofu is a high-protein food made from curdled soymilk that tastes bland and slightly nutty. It readily absorbs the flavors of the seasonings it is cooked with.

Tomatillo. Like tomatoes, tomatillos are fruits that are typically used in savory dishes. They resemble small green tomatoes and are covered by a thin, papery husk. They taste tart and tangy, with hints of apple, lemon, and pineapple.

Where to Find Ingredients

Local Suppliers

Asian Markets

coconut milk

enoki mushrooms

kombu

nori

tamarind pulp

young coconuts

Gourmet Stores

agar flakes

blue cornmeal

hearts of palm

porcini mushrooms

rice lasagna noodles

unsweetened soymilk

vanilla beans

Latin or Mexican Markets

ancho chiles

corn husks

epazote

masa harina

Online Suppliers

Beans and Grains

bulkfoods.com

naturalgrocers.com

purcellmountainfarms.com

ranchogordo.com

Nuts

nuts.com

sunorganic.com

Rice

lotusfoods.com

naturalgrocers.com

Spices

spicesinc.com

spicely.com

About the Author

Ramses Bravo is the executive chef at TrueNorth Health Center in Santa Rosa, California, where he has been delighting guests with healthful and delicious meals since 2007. He also has worked in numerous hotels and restaurants in California, Hawaii, and West Virginia. His extensive professional experience prepared him well for his unique position managing America's most wholesome kitchen.

In 1998 he graduated from City College in San Francisco with a degree in hotel and restaurant management. From there he went to the prestigious Greenbrier Resort in West Virginia and graduated from their three-year apprenticeship program. In 2002 Chef Bravo bid farewell to West Virginia and returned to California to become the executive chef for Kenwood Inn and Spa. The menus he designed there featured simple foods with bold flavors and were a big success. His four years at Kenwood Inn were the perfect preparation for his position at TrueNorth Health Center.

The recipes that Chef Bravo has developed do more than please palates. At TrueNorth, and now through this cookbook, they also serve as the foundation of dietary rebirth for people who want to transform their health.

Chef Bravo invites you to visit him at TrueNorth for a class, a meal, or a longer stay. Until then, keep up with his culinary adventures on Facebook. He hopes to see you soon!

Index

Recipe titles appear in *italics*.

A

acorn squash, in side dish, 76

addiction, to harmful foods, 4–6

agar/agar flakes, 124, 131

almonds, in dough, 35

American (U.S.) diet, 3, 5, 6

ancestors, harmful foods and, 4–5, 6

animal-based foods/protein

    ancestors and, 5

    food industry and, 6

    health related to, 3–4, 6–7

    preference for, 5

apple(s)

    -Mustard Dressing, 69

    -Pecan Cobbler, 128

    Slaw, Chayote-, 60

    -Strawberry Gelée, 123

    vs. oil/salt, 67

arterial health, 7

Arugula, Oven-Roasted Tomatoes with, 79

Asian Broth, 30

Asparagus Soup, Cream of, 46

atherosclerosis, animal-based products

    and, 4

autoimmune diseases, 10

avocado(s)

    -Corn Dressing, 71

    as energy food, 75

    fats and, 8

    in healthful diet, 10

    ripeness of, 71

B

baked dishes/recipes

    Bars, Banana-Pecan, 41

    Bars, Fig-Pecan, 126

    Cornmeal Loaf, Blue, 97

    Crust or Croutons, Polenta, 32–33

    "French Toast," Oatmeal, 40

    Plantains with Coconut-Vanilla Granola, 42

    Potatoes, Breakfast, 44

    Tofu Stir-Fry with Sweet-and-Sour Sauce, 108

    Yams and Mashed Potatoes, Twice-Baked, 81

Baked Rice Soup, Sea Vegetable and, 56

G

galangal, 132

garbanzo bean(s)

   Cooked, 31

   in hummus, 84, 121

   and Kale with Meyer Lemon and Parsley Dressing, 88

   Patties with Tomatillo Salsa, Forbidden Rice and, 100–101

garlic

   roasting, 25

   and Tamarind Glaze, Roasted, 116

   and Tamarind Glaze, Tofu and Tempeh Skewers with Roasted, 109

gelatin, agar as substitute for, 124, 131

Gelée, Apple-Strawberry, 123

ginger

   about, 132

   Dressing, Mango-, 68

   Sautéed Kale and Mushrooms with, 77

   Glaze, Roasted Garlic and Tamarind, 116

   Glaze, Tofu and Tempeh Skewers with Roasted Garlic and Tamarind, 109

gluten, 8, 95

grains

   as energy food, 75

   flour from, 8

   in healthful diet, 4, 10

   protein in, 7

   as staple food, 87

Granola, Baked Plantains with Coconut-Vanilla, 42

Granola, Coconut-Vanilla, 36

grapefruit, in salads, 59, 64

greens, 7, 8, 75

green vegetables, calcium in, 7

Grilled Ratatouille with Pesto Sauce, 80

grocery list, making, 12

H

harmful foods, addiction to, 4–6

Hawaiian Salad, 64

healthful living, 3

heart disease

   animal-based foods and, 4, 7

   salt (sodium) and, 8

   TrueNorth Health Center and, 10

hearts of palm, 132

Hearts of Palm Salad, 65